HAUNTED
GHOSTS AND THE PARANORMAL

REAL-LIFE GHOST ENCOUNTERS

JEFF BELANGER

ROSEN
PUBLISHING®

New York

This edition published in 2014 by:

The Rosen Publishing Group, Inc.
29 East 21st Street
New York, NY 10010

Library of Congress Cataloging-in-Publication Data

Belanger, Jeff.
Real-life ghost encounters/Jeff Belanger. — First Edition.
    pages cm. — (Haunted: ghosts and the paranormal)
Includes bibliographical references and index.
ISBN 978-1-4777-0678-7 (library binding)
1. Ghosts. 2. Haunted places. I. Title.
BF1461.B3865 2013
133.1—dc23

                                                    2012048803

Manufactured in the United States of America

CPSIA Compliance Information: Batch #S13YA: For further information, contact Rosen Publishing, New York, New York, at 1-800-237-9932.

First published as *Our Haunted Lives* by New Page Books/Career Press, copyright © 2006 by Jeff Belanger

For my sister,
Susan,
who is always good at talking to people.

Acknowledgments

This book simply would not exist without the people who agreed to be interviewed for it. To those who shared their very personal and profound experiences, I thank you for the trust you placed in me. And I thank you for standing up and furthering the discussion of the supernatural.

I'd like to thank author Studs Terkel for the inspiration on how to document people's life experiences and how to present them in book form. Terkel is a master of drawing out the story from the people he interviews, and I'm a big fan of his work.

Thank you to all of the people who helped me network with and contact witnesses of ghostly phenomena, especially Stephen Wagner from Paranormal.About.com.

Thank you to my editor, Christopher Carolei, for sharing the vision of how this book should come together, and thanks Michael Pye, Laurie Kelly-Pye, and Linda Rienecker for all that you do.

To my wife, Megan, who puts up with all of the oddities that come with having a job like mine. Her pride in me and her support of my writing continually pushes me to work harder and do better. (I guess after all of these years, I'm still trying to impress her.)

And thank you to the Ghostvillagers of the world. The people who have visited and contributed to my Web site, www.ghostvillage.com, have always inspired me. I appreciate their support and the global community they have created.

Contents

Introduction...9

Chapter 1: Haunted Homes 13

George Lutz, Amityville, New York   14

Aimee Wagner, Framingham, Massachusetts   33

Linda Dix, Toledo, Ohio   36

Tim Beauchamp, Grove, Oklahoma   39

Kim Strain, Sitka, Alaska   44

Janie Le'Kay, Birmingham, England   50

Sharon Moritz, Chicago, Illinois   56

Morris Sabanski, Toronto, Ontario, Canada   61

Chapter 2: Ghosts We Know 75

Rev. Father Scott E. Kingsbury, Los Angeles, California   76

William Gilbert, Brooksville, Florida   82

Lee Prosser, Foyil, Oklahoma   88

Robert Allen, Huron, South Dakota   92

Kathy Flaherty, Hog Island, Rhode Island   94

Jim Demick, Rockwood, Michigan   98

Heather Coker, New Palestine, Indiana   101

Sierra Gregoire, Benson, Vermont   105

Suzy Lehman, Jasper, Tennessee 108
Michael Wright, Salem, Virginia 112

Chapter 3: Ghosts on the Job 117
Jeff Revis, Dayton, Tennessee 118
William Zastrow, Austin, Texas 123
Jennifer Neighbor, Savannah, Georgia 127
Michael K. Mather, San Diego, California 131
Connie Cook, Las Vegas, Nevada 133
Bobby Mackey, Wilder, Kentucky 135

Chapter 4: Haunted Hotels and Inns........................141
Jaci Burkett, Gettysburg, Pennsylvania 142
Tom Haikin, Derby, England 148
Nora Quick, Albuquerque, New Mexico 152

Chapter 5: Near-Death Experience 159
Sandra Brooks, Clifton Forge, Virginia 160

Chapter 6: While You Were Sleeping 167
Jerry E. Spivey, Brooklyn, New York 168
Gino, Sterling Heights, Michigan 172
Ian Yeung, Thornhill, Ontario, Canada 177

Chapter 7: Ghost Hunting 181
Travis Hayes, North of Albany, Louisiana 182
John Zaffis, Stratford, Connecticut 186
Bill Jimenez, Ph.D., San Diego, California, and   192
      Pico Rivera, California

Chapter 8: Ghosts Out and About............................203
Erika Emal, Aix en Provence, France 204
Lokela Dakine, La'ie, Oahu, Hawaii 208

Glossary 214

For More Information...216

For Further Reading..218

Index 220

Introduction

When I started writing about ghosts and the supernatural, I began with some of the most famous haunted places. The Tower of London, the White House, Archer Avenue in Chicago, and Gettysburg were all certainly high on my "supernatural radar." I was intrigued by the history, stirred by the legends, but completely gripped by the first-hand accounts I heard from the many witnesses of supernatural events at these renowned haunts.

Through the years, I've spoken with many hundreds of people who have shared their very personal and profound spiritual experiences with me—from encounters with strange cold spots, unexplained knocks, disembodied voices, even detailed conversations with relatives who have passed on. I have heard conviction in the voices that told me about their brush with the other side, and I've seen the wonder that returns to the witness's eyes as they recount the incredible events they've experienced.

For centuries, ghost experiences were told and retold by oral tradition. Even today—in a world that chronicles almost every event no matter how mundane via photograph, video, audio, and/or written word—details of ghostly encounters are still spread mainly by word-of-mouth. But that trend is changing. Today, belief in the existence of ghostly phenomena is on the rise, and some people are willing to come forward and share their own stories on television programs, radio call-in shows, and Internet sites. These people are quickly finding they aren't alone.

Real-Life Ghost Encounters is all about the experience, that life-altering event that proves—at least to the witness—that there is indeed life beyond death. This is a collection of my very spirited conversations with people who have experienced ghosts. Some of the encounters are frightening, some are touching, and some are simply quirky—it seems the other side also has a sense of humor.

These accounts are presented in the words of the eyewitnesses. Every effort was made to preserve the nature, nuances, and dialogue of each interview, because I want you to know these people. Understand that no one was placed on the hot seat with a lone spotlight shining on them. These are conversations.

You'll notice that some of the grammar may not be perfect. We ask that you forgive both the author and editor, but this is how people talk. It doesn't make them ignorant or even uneducated; we simply don't speak the way we write. If you were going to an important job interview, you would likely wear your best business attire, you'd sit with your back straight, and you'd carefully answer each question in an articulate manner. Though this is putting on your best face and placing your best foot forward, is it the real you? No, it's the polished and careful you. The real you is that person on the couch in sweatpants on a rainy Saturday morning. And if we could stay with the couch analogy for just a minute longer, now imagine how that person in sweats speaks. Imagine you had a friend come over—the kind of friend you know well enough that you don't have to change out of your sweatpants for. Your dialogue with that person would be relaxed. Some English snobs may say "lazy," but I would call it "intimate." And though William Strunk and E.B. White might have cringed while reading an exact transcript of two friends talking, the reality is that the language works. Information and meaning are shared and understood, and the content is genuine. There's beauty in that.

Writing on the supernatural often falls victim to sensationalism. One objective with *Real-Life Ghost Encounters* was to deliver each witness's account with as few distractions as possible and spotlight these real people who experienced something profound. This is what happened, in their own words, just as they would tell it to a close friend. I tried to make the interviews as informal as possible. I wanted people comfortable—in their sweatpants, if you will. My goal in presenting each interview was simply to stay out of the way of their experiences and to not judge or even comment on what was being said. After all, I wasn't there. I can't prove nor disprove something I didn't personally witness.

One thing I've noticed throughout the years, and especially while working on this book, is that it is a cathartic release for witnesses when they discuss their experiences. "The truth will set you free," as the Bible says in John 8:32. I could hear more than one sigh of relief as people began to tell their stories. There was laughter at times, sometimes from the sheer discomfort of saying something that may be construed as strange or impossible. In other cases, the laughter and smiles were genuine in reflecting on an event or period in one's life. Sometimes there were tears. Not only were these experiences personal, but they often involved the death of a loved one—an incident that was sometimes relived in relaying a series of events.

A perfectly valid question to ask is, "How do I know these people are telling the truth?" A good question—and a question with a fuzzy answer at best. What is truth? That's a question philosophers have been trying to answer for centuries. In one regard, truth is relative. Speak to any devoutly religious person about what *truth* is, and he or she will likely quote from one of his or her religious texts. He or she may believe the text and its teachings to be truth. But is it universal truth? No, because there are a great many belief systems on our tiny planet, and so far, none of them has been able to capture 100 percent of the marketshare of believers. One *truth* doesn't speak to all people.

Do you trust your own senses? Most of us do. And the people interviewed in this book do as well. Some used to say, "I won't believe it unless I see it," and see it they did. There was truth and conviction in the retelling.

One aspect of the ghost experience that has captivated me more than any other is that they cross all geographic boundaries. They're in religious texts and history books, and there's a term for "ghost" in every language. Ghosts are a sign of something else being out there beyond our traditional understanding of the world. They force us to question our own mortality and to explore our own deeper understanding of spirituality.

You'll notice that some of the people being interviewed had their experiences many decades ago. You may ask if their memory can be trusted. You may be surprised at the great detail in which these witnesses recall their ghost encounters. Do you remember what you got for a present on your fifth birthday? Probably not. But do you remember your child being born? The death of a loved one? Your wedding day? These are profound events, and they've been burned into your long-term memory. The ghost encounter is no different. Whether 5 years or 50 years have gone by, the experience is still vivid.

As people shared their stories with me, I tried to ask the questions you might have asked regarding the details of the event, and how it may have changed or touched their lives. You're invited to sit in on these conversations.

In the pages that follow, I'd like you to meet some good people. Some are young, some are much older. They're your sisters, your brothers, your neighbors, and your friends. In many ways, they're us, too.

Chapter 1

Haunted Homes

Photo credit: istockphoto.com/Rob Zeiler

Our home is our castle, the place we (hopefully) feel the safest, and it's where we can be ourselves. After living in a house, apartment, or dormitory for even a short period of time, we quickly get used to the various noises the building makes, the neighbors who come and go at various hours, or the way the heater makes the wall tick, tick, tick. We also know the way the rooms in our homes feel. So when something strange is going on, many times the homeowner or tenant is the person who notices first. Because we get acclimated to a building, if something is off, even by a little bit, we can sense it.

Haunted homes are often frightening because people are dealing with an intruder—sometimes an intruder who can't be seen, or in more profound haunting cases, it's an intruder who can be seen, but one who can't be touched, let alone handcuffed.

There's a myriad of reasons why a ghost or spirit may stick around a home. Perhaps the ghost is simply a psychic impression left in the building—one that some people are able to tune in to. Another theory is that the spirit may not realize they are dead, and so they simply hang around where they were most comfortable. On the darker side of the supernatural, some speculate that houses or people might be plagued with demons or other evil forces that are trying to torment and drive them away. No matter the cause, when someone is dealing with a haunting in his or her home, it can be both frustrating and frightening.

George Lutz
Amityville, New York
Autumn 1975

On Wednesday, November 14, 1974, around 3 a.m., 23-year-old Ronald "Butch" DeFeo, Jr., sat awake in his bedroom at 112 Ocean Avenue in Amityville, New York. DeFeo, wrought with emotional and drug problems, sat seething as his mother, father, two brothers, and two sisters all lay sleeping in their beds in the silence of that cold autumn night. Butch reached for a .35-caliber Marlin rifle he kept hidden, and he walked out of his room toward the bedroom where his parents were sleeping. He slipped in, aimed the rifle at his father first, and fired twice. Next he shot his mother twice, leaving both parents in pools of blood. Over the next several minutes, he systematically executed every member of his family, sealing his name in the halls of infamy.

One might ask, "Who would ever want to live in a house where such an atrocity happened?" It's an easy question to ask when you're not currently trying to buy a house, but what if you needed a home for your family, you've already looked at dozens of houses, and you find a wonderful home for a significantly undervalued price? What if it's been a year since the brutal murder, and you and your family agree that "houses don't have memories"?

The Amityville house is one of the most famous haunting cases in the world. Ronald DeFeo's brutality captivated Americans for a brief moment, but mass murderers are soon forgotten as another twisted monster comes along, ups the ante, and makes us all forget about the last one. But we didn't forget the house. 112 Ocean Avenue still captivates us—but not so much because of what Ronald DeFeo did there, but because of the supernatural, and by some accounts, demonic events that George Lutz and his family went through for 28 days after they moved in.

George and Kathy Lutz were married in July of 1975. Both had been married before, and Kathy had children from her previous marriage. They decided to sell both of their houses and combine households. Kathy's house sold first, so the Lutzes all packed into George's Long Island home until they could find something suitable for all of them. What George Lutz experienced in the autumn of 1975 has profoundly affected the rest of his life.

How long did it take to find a new home after you and Kathy moved in together?

We looked at about 50 homes over the months that we decided to combine the households. We had actually gone to contract on another home about a month before we found the Amityville house. That one was on the water, it was in Lindenhurst, and it had a boathouse. It was smaller than this house, it needed repairs that the sellers were not willing to negotiate with—the boathouse needed dredging to get the boat in, the roof needed replacing, and that fell through. When that fell apart we just kept looking. We found the Amityville house, if I recall correctly, from an ad in the paper. We found a Realtor and she said, "Look, I want to show you this house—this is how the other half of Amityville looks"—because we were looking everywhere we could. I had a boat and I had dockage fees, and when you added that into the mortgages we had on both houses, it gave us an idea of how much we were spending then. We felt that we could combine the homes, get something on the water, and have our own boathouse and not spend all that time traveling back and forth to the boathouse.

So the Realtor showed us the house. When she showed it to us she said before we went, she said, "I don't know if I should tell you now or after you've seen the house, but this was the house that the DeFeo murders took place in." We kind of looked at each other like, "I'm not sure what you're talking about." And then she reminded us about Ronald DeFeo having killed his whole family. That had been in the newspapers about a year before. If I recall correctly, this was sometime maybe late August or September, some place in there. We saw the house and as soon as Kathy walked in she just started smiling. This was the best one that she had seen so far in terms of what she liked and what we were looking for. As I remember now, it was a bright sunny day, we had the kids with us, we walked through it, and we all really fell in love with it.

We went home and talked about it for days. We talked about the price, how this could possibly work, what kind of mortgage we would need, what kind of payments we were looking at, the taxes, insurance costs—all of the different things you do when you decide to buy a house. And we spent a lot of time with the children individually and together talking about whether they would want to live in that house.

Did the children have any concerns at all?

In the first movie that was done about this, James Brolin says something to the effect of, "houses don't have memories." And I think that's the way we thought, without a doubt. It never occurred to us that it would be uninhabitable. We had concern for the kids—there's going to be some notoriety about this, and we were concerned about them. You don't just force your kids to move into a place like this, that isn't how we did things. But they had no reservations, they had no problems, and we went back at least two more times. We drove around the town a little bit, around the neighborhood, and we spent more time looking through the house. Eventually we made an offer.

I don't remember the specifics because it's been a long time, but I'm pretty sure they were looking for $90,000 and we offered $80,000 and they took it. One way to describe this is that the house was probably worth somewhere around $110,000. They hadn't been able to sell it since they had put it up for sale about a year earlier and the estate was willing to bargain about it. So we made an offer of $80,000 and we went and got a mortgage from the first bank we went to, and the mortgage was $60,000. We had more than enough cash to close on the difference—from the two sales of our houses. We packed up our stuff and the moving date was set.

We closed on the house the day of the move. My house was sold and we had no place to go other than there—everything was in trucks, and on trailers, and in vans and we had friends helping us move. We went into the title company and we met our lawyer and their lawyer there, and we do up all of the documents. We got down to the house and we find we didn't have the key. So we had to go find the realtor and get a key. Other than that, the only other thing that went wrong that comes to mind is that when I told a friend of mine who I built motorcycles with and rode with what house we were buying, he absolutely insisted I get the house blessed. He was such a good friend and I had never seen him do this kind of thing or say this kind of thing before. So I complied.

Did you have someone specific in mind to bless the house?

I asked Kathy about it because I wasn't Catholic. She explained to me that you get a priest to come out and he blesses the house for you. I said, "Okay, if that's what Jimmy wants, that's what we'll do."

A year and a half before, I had been married, and that ended up in a divorce and then in annulment proceedings. I was invited down to the diocesan offices in Rockville Center to meet with an official of the diocese. His name was Father Ralph Pecoraro. "Father Ray" we called him. He spent time with me to explain the process—I was a Methodist, so this was new and foreign to me at the time. We struck up a friendship, and from time to time we would talk, which was really strange for me. I was a biker, I wasn't a Catholic, but something about this guy made him different from most people you meet. He was more than just special; he was worth spending time with. He would take my calls and I would take his. It wasn't like there was a lot of this, but we stayed in touch. I called him because he was the only priest I could think of. I called him and said, "Would you come out and bless the house? We bought this house, and Kathy would like this done, and it's been suggested that we do this." He said, "Sure, I'd be glad to."

I had no idea he was not a parish priest, I had no idea that he was an ecclesiastical judge for the tribunal there, that he had an STL [Licentiate in Sacred Theology] degree, which is the equivalent of a law degree, that he spoke so many languages, or any number of other things about him. He was just somebody that I liked. I asked him and he said, "Sure, I'd be glad to," and he showed up shortly after we got the key and were in the process of moving in. I waved, he waved, and he went on in the house and went about blessing it.

When he was done, I tried to pay him and he wouldn't take money. He said, "You don't charge for this, and you don't charge friends for this." I thought that was a very kind thing to say, and then he said, "You know, I felt something really strange in that one upstairs bedroom," and he described the bedroom. And we said that's what we were going to use as a sewing room, we're not going to use it as a bedroom. He said, "That's good, as long as no one sleeps in there, that's fine." And that's all he said and he left.

So that was move-in day, and that's the priest leaving.

Were there any problems that first night?

I couldn't get warm, but that was probably from working so much outside. As we unloaded stuff, I took the cardboard boxes and put them in the fireplace and burned them. And I made an intense enough fire that I blew out the fireproof glass. They were pretty surprised when I finally got another piece for it. What was really interesting was that I had to go way out to the other end of Long Island to get a piece of this glass specifically cut. It wasn't like you go down to the hardware store and get one of these. And they said, "How did you ever do this?" I said it was a pretty intense fire, but I never thought this would happen. It actually blew out and shattered.

At what point do you start to notice that something doesn't seem right in the house?

There were a few things when you look back. There were so many different things that when I look back at it, and when I try to describe it, what happens for you is that you start to question your own thoughts, you question what's going on, and you don't have the answers.

We found there were cold spots. There was one in the stair-way, there was one in the basement, and there was one out in the boathouse. We would walk through the house and they would be there. The one in the boathouse was pretty solid, you'd turn around and there it was. The one in the basement, as I recall, wasn't always there. There would be times when you were look-ing for it and it wouldn't be there. As time goes on, you start to wonder what these things are, where is this draft coming from? You start to notice that there is a deadness of sound. You would walk into the living room and you would walk out to the front porch, which was a sunroom all enclosed, it faced the street, and you would see cars go past but you wouldn't hear them. And that was pretty weird.

You know how sometimes when there's been a lot of yelling in the room, the resonance changes—you know, how your voice sounds? The living room always sounded that way. It was, like, dead. But you don't notice that right away. It just sticks with you after a while.

I'd be lying in bed and I'd hear the front door slam shut. It's an unmistakable sound in that house. You absolutely knew that was the front door. I'd go downstairs and the dog would be asleep at the door and nothing would be disturbed, it would still be locked. So you start questioning yourself that way.

Were other people in the family hearing the door, too?

I don't think so when I think back about it. There were a number of times I would think a clock radio or something went off downstairs. I heard what I can only term as a marching band tuning up, and at one time it had sounded like they had rolled up the carpet there were so many footsteps down there. So much noise. And you go running downstairs to see what it is or what caused this, and you get to the landing halfway down and there's nothing, and the dog would be asleep. And he was a young black lab and they're hyper—they just don't sleep through stuff, they wake up.

At different times I can still remember looking at him saying, "Some watchdog you're turning out to be." [*Laughs.*] His name was Harry. And Harry lived for a number of years out in California and eventually in Arizona. He was a really cool dog.

So was this thing kind of singling you out in the house?

No, because one of the things that happens with this stuff is that you think it's all about you. You think it's all going on just for you, and Kathy and I had such a good relationship that we were able to openly discuss stuff without worrying what the other would think. That's one of those things…when you find that you keep it if you can. So we would try to communicate some of this stuff. I think that was a really good part of survival for this and for getting out of there eventually.

Kathy turned into an old woman there. She would feel someone come up behind her and embrace her. She would smell this perfume that was, forgive the expression, "old lady" perfume. She would feel embraced, and it would be comforting. And she would explain that, and that's chilling. That's not something that she had ever gone through before. When she turned into an old woman, she didn't just age a little, she aged a lot. She turned into someone completely different physically than I had ever thought was possible. Her mother saw this, and years later we were asked if we would do lie detector tests, and that was certainly one of the questions we wanted covered and had put on the test. This happened even after we moved out of the house, this also happened at her mom's house.

And this was all in the span of just a few weeks?

Yes.

Was there indeed a hidden room in the basement?

I was at work, and Kathy called me and said that she had just found this room, it was painted red, and behind the bookcase. She was working in the basement and was putting things away in the living room, and she went to see if this bookcase was movable. I guess she had gone to put things on it and it had moved and behind it was this—I don't know how to describe it other than as a *room*. It's a space—you had to crouch down to get in there. This was under the stairs in the basement and it was all painted red. It was hidden behind this bookcase. It was never shown to us when we saw the house.

Was the bookcase there from the DeFeos?

As far as we know. It was there when we took possession of the house—forgive that expression. So she called me about this and eventually we managed to find the house plans—the as-builts for the house. The district attorney still had them, and we went and got them and this place, this area, this room, did not show up there.

How big of a space are we talking? Could you get inside?

Oh yes, you could fit two very friendly people maybe, sitting down. The fact that it was painted red, the fact that it had odors coming out of it—and the odors weren't always there. And there was no pipe access for sewers or anything like that. We took Harry down there and he just wouldn't go in, he backed away. It's the only time I can recall him ever cowering from something. That was just one of those discoveries—one of those things in the first few weeks after moving in.

Our daughter, Missy, you'd walk past her room and she would be talking, and singing, and playing in her room and happy as anything. She'd walk out of the room and stop singing. She'd go back in the room and start singing again. She asked her mom at one point, "Do angels talk?" Another time she started talking about this angel like it was a friend of hers, and it had a name—its name was Jody.

How old was Missy at the time?

I want to say 4 years old. She was at an age where she could converse. When they hit 4, it's really cool because they can talk with you and communicate.

At what point do things start getting bad?

This is not bad; this is just a series of events. This isn't what you call "bad." So much of my memory goes back to after we left the house and what we discovered after leaving and talking. Forgive my way of putting this, but one of the things we always thought about it after we left was that the house didn't want to let you leave. Things like going someplace, getting out of there, me going to work, things like that. One of the things that Kathy had done was join a local high school class to learn how to reupholster. We had bought the DeFeo's dining room set—it was better than anything we had—and Kathy had wanted to reupholster the chairs. She had signed up for this class, paid for it, gone out and bought the fabric, then never went to a single class.

I think you can guess from us having a room called the sewing room what kind of stuff she liked doing. We had a bedspread that Kathy had made from remnants of velvet, and she put this pattern together and it was on the bed. There's a picture of that as we left the house. Years later someone came to us and said, "You know what that pattern is?" We said we had no idea; it's just the way it worked out from the pieces she had. They said, "Well, it's a harlequin pattern used during Lent mostly in the New Orleans area." It's to ward off evil during Lent, supposedly.

And it was random chance that that's how the pattern came together?

It's a strange thing for somebody to say to you. It's just one of those things you put on the list to remember if you can.

I very rarely went to work after a while. I would phone it in, so to speak. I'd go in to make sure the payroll got done, or go in for only a couple hours. It wasn't the 60-hour weeks I used to work.

Did you experience a depression, or you just didn't want to leave the house?

I got very sick and lost a lot of weight there. Part of it was I just didn't want to leave the house. Kathy described it later as: "the house was charming." We would invite people over instead of going to see them. Friends. There came a point when we invited people over to see whether we were crazy or not. Because when they sat in the kitchen and they could hear the steps of people walking around upstairs after the kids had been put to bed, and we all went upstairs to see that there was no way it was the kids. When they confirmed that for you, you almost want to break down and say out loud, "I'm not crazy. They hear it too."

That is such an emotional moment when someone else confirms for you that what you're hearing is not just you hearing it. It's not your imagination. This is not a play on something going on in your own mind. One of the things that occurred to us after we left too was the thoughts that would come. You knew that these thoughts were not your own. This is not how you ever thought about things, or other people, or events. These are not nice things; this is not nice stuff to talk about.

Were they violent thoughts?

I'm going to leave it at the way I said it. And you would know this, and you would start questioning what is going on with me that I would even think this.

So this was a way you've never felt before?

We're not talking about feelings, we're not talking about thoughts. We're talking about thinking a particular thing that is just not part of your own nature, your own makeup as you know yourself to be. This was not normal. This would happen, and when it would happen, you'd start to wonder. Forget about if you want to call it sanity. So much of that dissipated and went away after leaving. Not immediately, but it certainly did diminish. One of the things that we learned that works for that is humor. You have to find something to think about that is positive and funny for that to lose some of its power.

It's not like just thinking nice things, it comes easier with time, but it's such a hard thing to describe, and yet it was a direct result of living there. From those kinds of things you start to get a feel of what might have gone on before we were there. You start to get an idea of what kinds of influences may have caused what went on there before.

A friend of ours came over with a friend of hers. She was my tenant, and she invited a guy that she knew had lived in a haunted house. And he came over and told us what he had learned to do, and that was to go through the house and bless it. In other words, say the Lord's Prayer in each room, open a window, and command whatever was there to leave in the name of Jesus Christ. You get done, you go around and close the windows, and the house would be cleansed. I said to myself, you know we've already had this place blessed, but if this is going to work, okay. So we did that.

We did it twice. The first time we did it, Danny, our oldest boy's hands got caught in the window with pressure being put down on his hands. And they blew up. His hands got really large and swollen, he was screaming. It took quite a bit of pressure to get the window off of his hands. You could never explain how it happened because it's not the kind of window to just slam up and down. We had sent the kids around to close the windows and lock them. We get our coats on to go to the hospital, we're at the door to leave, and Danny stops crying. We look at his hands and they're fine.

We did it again. We heard this chorus of voices saying, "Will you stop?" One memory of it is, "Will you please stop?" Another memory of it is, "Will you stop?" Either way, when that happened, you got the sense that this is not going to work.

At what point do you seek outside help?

The second time we did that. That night was worse. It was reported years later that there was no storm outside, but for the five of us in the house there certainly was. I was lying in bed and everyone was asleep, and Kathy lifts up off the bed and starts to slide away from the bed, away from me. I feel something get in the bed with us. I'm unable to move, I hear the kids' beds continually slamming up and down on the floor and being dragged. We heard these pigeons on the air conditioner top overhead from the master bath, and they're fluttering all night long, keeping me awake, and yet there are no pigeons there the next morning—or any nest or anything like that. The lights flickered. We brought the dog up to stay right by the bedroom. We tied him right to the doorknob and he's up and going in circles and throwing up all night.

The boys came down in the morning absolutely frightened. They were unable to get down to me and I was unable to get up to them. Missy came in and just asked, "What was that all about?" The boys asked, "What was that all about." Kathy had no memory of much of it. That day we spent trying to get a hold of Father Ray, and he said all the right words.

We didn't get up to leave that morning, you need to understand that. This was our house, we lived there. We didn't know what was going on, but he said the right words. He said something to the effect of, "Look, you guys obviously need some sleep. Is there someplace you can go just for the night?" And Kathy said her mom's house. He said, "That's perfect, why don't you just go there and get some sleep and we'll talk some more." How he said it were just the right words to get us out. And her mom was wonderful, she said, "Absolutely, come on over."

When we left, we didn't know we weren't coming back. We didn't know that what we were leaving behind we would never see again.

We had one hell of a ride getting to her mom's house. We had all kinds of problems. We both levitated there. The first night we were there, the dog was tied to the piano and he dragged it across the room. The kids fought in their sleep for weeks and they fought the memories and the nightmares from living there. I'm leaving so much out… the point of all of this is we knew that one night wasn't going to do it, and we needed to know what was going on and how to fix this. We also felt very strongly that whatever had gone on before we were there, Ronald DeFeo needed psychological help. There was no doubt in our minds that he was influenced by what was in that house, and that meant that the conviction for the six murders, and being declared sane, that shouldn't be allowed. We should try to do something about that. So through friends of ours, they contacted his attorney and we met with him to talk about that.

What did he say?

He told us a number of strange stories about the housekeeper for the DeFeo family, and different evidence that had taken place over the years that he had heard about. He brought back a criminologist—a guy that was supposedly a criminologist—he turned out to be a writer named Paul Hoffman, who eventually wrote an article about us in *Good Housekeeping* magazine, of course without our permission. We met with him three, maybe four times, and he sent over a contract that was about 40 pages. He wanted us to give his corporation the house—donate it; swear that everything that we said was the truth, take lie-detector tests from whoever he chose, and if we failed the tests, we forfeited the house and rights to our own story. He offered us a percentage of whatever he managed to make into a movie or a book, and in there was also a payment percentage of proceeds to go to Ronald DeFeo.

I guess you don't need a lawyer to help you with that decision.

No. A friend of ours was a representative for textbooks, and he looked at this and said, "I'll get you someone," and he immediately got a hold of someone at Prentice-Hall and set up a meeting and we went to that. And the fellow at Prentice-Hall who became our editor recommended this writer by the name of Jay Anson, and that's how that came about.

Why tell your story? Why go public?

I like that question. And the reason I like it is because it's days like the last few months [*referring to the April 2005 release of MGM's new version of the movie,* The Amityville Horror] have held that bring back the memories of why we did that, and they bring them back so strongly that the conviction has to stay for it to be valid now as well. In March of '76, I think it was March 6th, a news crew, a number of psychics, Ed and Lorraine Warren [*paranormal investigators*], Mary Downey [*psychic*], a photographer, representatives from what we thought was Duke University's psychical research center, came at different times during the day, and most of them stayed overnight in the house. They did a full investigation and a number of séances, or at least one, while they were there. The consensus of opinion from the experts was that whatever it is there never walked the face of the earth in human form. That they could not clean the house, they could not fix it. If the house was to be fixed, it would require an Anglican or Roman Catholic priest to come and say Mass there. He would not be a normal priest; he would have to be one that was reserved for such things,

I would guess mostly sequestered. He would have to fast before he went in, and in no uncertain terms, his life would be put in jeopardy by trying to cast out what was there.

The other part of the summation that usually gets left out of any explanation about it is that it wasn't limited to just this one entity, but there were other forms of activity that were caused by other forms of energy. I heard it put one time that this was like a supermarket of these kinds of entities, or phenomena, if you will. And your own personal sensitivity might be the trigger that makes you aware of some of this, someone else with a different makeup or psychological makeup, or nature, or whatever might not experience anything there. The house found certain people interesting and others not. It liked being fed by people, it liked having people come over there to choose from and play with. There were people involved with trying to help us from a distance that were affected by this. The only people that we know of that still live in the same place that they did then is the Warrens. No one else.

So why go public with your story?

Oh yeah, thanks. Yeah, let's stick to the point. None of us went back with them when they went to the house. We weren't going to interfere and we weren't going to tell them what happened—we wanted them to tell us. So they went in really cold, so cold that it was annoying in many ways to Ed [*Warren*], because I just wouldn't talk about it with them and neither would Kathy. It was only after they were there, it was only after they had done this, that we told them what happened.

Ed wasn't necessarily enthusiastic about the others who were also investigating, but he didn't fight me about it. I just wanted more documentation, not just theirs. It wasn't a question of not trusting them; I just wanted this fixed. We were going to move back in there. All our stuff is there—this is our house. My boats and motorcycles, everything is there.

We spoke with the Warrens at length, and we started to learn some of what they had spent so many years doing, and the effects that this has on families, and why people don't talk about it because you hold yourself up for ridicule. Most of the time the documentation of the history, for example, is lost as are the people willing to stand up on their own that were involved in some manner and say, "This is what happened to me there."

We felt at that point that we have a choice. And you need to understand that DeFeo's attorney had [publicized] us. He had called a press conference, he told us that our children would be bothered by the newspapers at their new schools and from their grandmother's house if we didn't agree to do this press conference. Never did we realize that he made all this up and newspapers don't do that kind of thing. He had done this for his own purposes, he had gone and appeared at the house on camera, he called a news crew there, and he had agreed that he would never do that.

We knew we couldn't move back in the house, and we also knew we couldn't ask a priest to come and put his life on the line for a piece of property, and we knew that the newspapers had it and weren't going to let go of it. So we had a choice. We decided it's our story, this is what happened, we're either going to stand up and say it happened or we're going to try and become anonymous someplace else, but in any case we were leaving New York and were going to do this. We're going to sell my business, we're going to leave everything that's there and deal with that later, and we're moving out-of-state. It was a choice to make. I can't say it was the wisest choice, and I can't say that if I had known all of the controversy, all of the accusations, all of the legal problems…there's been something like at least 13 lawsuits about this, and all of them involve one thing or another, and that is the right to tell even one single day of our own story ourselves. If I had known all of the different things that would've gone on after, I don't know that we would've done this.

I can't blame anyone that goes through this kind of thing to never speak of it again.

When did things start to calm down after leaving the house? Is there a point where you kind of felt life was getting normal again?

Yeah, this morning when I was moving furniture. [*Laughs.*]

Today was the day, huh?

[*Laughs.*] There is no day that comes to mind. One of the ways we described it was like it had a half-life, and as time went on, it would be less and less. Less intrusive. One of the things you're really afraid of doing is blaming everything that goes wrong in your life on the house forever. You can't do that.

When did you know you and your family would be okay?

We get on a plane, we give the car, and the keys, and the title—we give it to the guy that helped us unload the bags. We said, "Here, we ain't comin' back. You can have it." We get on the plane with the dog, we have a few suitcases, and we land in San Diego, Mother's Day, 1976. We're going to start over. I've got my business sold to the first guy that comes in, looks at it, and makes an offer. I sold it for maybe 10 to 20 percent of what it was really worth, but I was going. Either way, I was closing the doors and leaving. We get out of the plane, we're in the airport, the kids are walking Harry over across to us while we're waiting for the rental car to show up. It's really early morning, it's like six in the morning or so, and the dog is walking sideways because he had to be drugged to get on the plane. And Kathy and I are just laughing. The sun is out, the grass is green, it's so gorgeous, the birds are singing, and the kids are walking this half-drunk dog across the walkway, and we were just laughing that we were able to do this. That we got this far.

That's the beginning of getting away.

George Lutz passed away suddenly on the afternoon of May 8, 2006. This was one of the last major interviews Lutz gave about his experiences in Amityville.

Aimee Wagner
Framingham, Massachusetts
November 2004

Horace Mann Hall is a three-story brick dormitory building named after the founder of Framingham State College. Inside Mann Hall's lobby/common room, I sat down with Aimee Wagner, a 22-year-old senior from East Bridgewater, Massachusetts. Framingham State has a few ghostly legends attached to it, some of which Aimee has experienced personally.

When did you first hear about the ghosts here?

When we came for orientation, a lot of people who do orientation with the new students tell the story about it. This school used to teach teachers, and it was primarily women up until the 1970s, which is when they first started allowing men in. For a long time, the buildings were Horace Mann, Peirce, which is the dorm right next door, and Crocker Hall is the building right here [*points to a building a short distance away*], which form this little triangle.

Peirce was actually built over the remains of another building that had burned down. Connecting these three buildings are tunnels. They had the tunnels so the women wouldn't have to go outside in the inclement weather. You can still walk in them… you can if you're sneaky. The tunnels were closed off because supposedly there was a fire down there because of faulty wiring or something—I'm not exactly sure what—and a girl died. She was one of the young women who came here. No one that I've ever known has ever called her by any name, but that's the story that goes around campus.

What ghostly activity do people claim to experience?

I've heard people say they feel like someone else is in the room in various rooms here [*Mann Hall*] and in Peirce. People have had things misplaced—not anything really big. Not a lot of people talk about it because if you tell your friends, they're kind of like, "Yeah, okay, whatever."

Supposedly, a few years ago there was an R.A. [*resident assistant*] that moved in during the summer a couple weeks before the students came back, and she was checking out all the rooms. I'm pretty sure this happened on the third floor of Peirce. She had the mirrors up against the wall outside of the rooms, and she was the only one in the building that night. When she woke up in the morning and came outside, all of the mirrors had been turned around to face the other way. And she could verify that she was the only person in the building at the time. The mirrors were facing the wall originally and when she looked the next morning, the mirrors were facing out.

I used to live over in the third floor of Peirce. It was a strange place to be—it was oppressive at times. Not necessarily like something was going to come and get you, but there was definitely somebody else there, though you couldn't see them. Sometimes when you woke up at night it would be a little creepy. The single rooms over there aren't very big. The way my room was set up was basically like a closet—it was almost the size of a walk-in closet. The room was kind of long and narrow and had a high ceiling. I would wake up or come into the room at different times, and it got to the point where I would check under my bed or check behind the clothes in my closet. It was very weird. I would come into the room and feel like someone was already in the room. I just felt distinctively that there was somebody else there and it was definitely a female. I didn't feel like they were angry or had evil intent or anything like that.

Did you discuss your feelings with any of your neighbors in the hall?

I didn't talk about it too much again because it's kind of an odd thing to bring up—did you feel something weird in your room last night? Because I know I did. [*Laughs.*]

The strangest thing that ever happened to me personally happened one morning after I just woke up. It was a typical day, I think it was November, and right across from my old room was the bathroom. So I went into the bathroom and I was washing my face and everything, and I looked up and I saw there was a red handprint on my arm—the mark was almost to the point of bruising. I had a short-sleeved shirt on, so I could see everything. And I thought maybe I had slept like this [*she places her hand on her upper arm*], or slept on my side and held it and it made an imprint. But I knew it couldn't have been an imprint from my blanket or my clothes because you could see each finger pad; it was very, very distinct.

So I put my own hand over it to see if it was mine, and the fingers were much longer than mine. And also you can see that I have a crooked middle finger [*she holds up her hand to show her middle finger is crooked at the tip*], and the finger that was on my arm wasn't crooked so it couldn't have been mine. It's a pretty weird story, and I've only told a couple of people.

I went back to my room where I had a disposable camera, and I tried to take a picture of it, but the picture came out blurry because it was just the cheap disposable. I tried to show people, I said, "Look at this." Some people believed me and other people thought I was crazy. The handprint was gone by that night.

The night this happened I had slept through the night just fine—there wasn't anything strange going on. I actually called my mom. I said, "Mom, I woke up and this happened."

What did your mother say?

She believed me. She thought it was really weird and said this place is definitely haunted—but she thought it was kind of a strange building anyway.

Linda Dix
Toledo, Ohio
Summer of 1997

Linda Dix is a 51-year-old certified mental health nurse. She believes her house in Toledo has been haunted for quite some time. The house was built in 1907 on land where an old farmhouse once stood. When one person witnesses a supernatural event, the impact is profound. When multiple people witness the same event and can verify that each saw the same thing, the impression is compounded. In the summer of 1997, Linda, her husband, J.R., and grandson, Jacob, witnessed an invisible playmate.

Why do you think your house is haunted?

Because we've always had strange things happen here, and we've heard strange noises. We even put flour down on the floor to see if we could catch footprints, and we got footprints one time in the flour.

Were they barefoot prints or were they shoes?

They were shoes, little tiny shoes. I had children at the time who were 12 and 16, and these did not fit their shoes. We kept hearing footsteps in the night and stuff. My husband and I thought it was our kids doing it, so we put this stuff down on the floor thinking we could catch them, and what we got were little tiny footprints of about maybe a 7- or 8-year old.

We thought it was our kids. You know, you have a 16-year-old son who likes to stay out at night—and we thought that's what the racket was going up and down the stairs with him sneaking out. Or maybe that our daughter at 12 was sneaking out.

Guests stay over at the house, and we have to warn them that sometimes our spirits like to make their presence known, so don't get freaked out because you may have the sensation of someone jumping on your bed and nobody is there. Or the covers being pulled off, or articles of clothing being hid, and when you tell them. "Okay, put them back." The things miraculously reappear back where you thought you left them in the first place. We've watched cups go flying off the top of the refrigerator; we've had several people over when that happened. The cups ended up on the other side of the room and you say, "Okay, we know that you're here."

Ever since our grandson Jacob was about 18 months old, he would point and say, "The boy." And he would point to the ceiling, or anywhere, which I thought was strange at the time. He'd point at the light on the ceiling and say, "The boy." So we thought it was just imagination or what have you.

What happened in the summer of 1997?

Jacob was about four then. We brought him back some toys from Gettysburg—a set of Civil War plastic army men. He has gone with us a lot of times to Gettysburg—that's one of his favorite places too, but we had just got that for him. He set this out on the coffee table and would play a lot. And we always heard him talking to things.

A lot of weird things happened here, but that one was kind of unique because we thought he had an imaginary friend like a lot of children do, but then we actually saw the pieces moving—you know, soldiers were falling down and different things like that. My husband and I were watching TV, and Jacob sat at one end of the coffee table and he appeared to be talking to someone at the other end of the table. At first we thought maybe he's hitting the table, and that's doing it.

So we watched a little bit closer. But his body wouldn't be touching the table, and the things would still move. He moved his toy and a piece on the other side of the table would move. It's like there's something else going on here. And then we asked him, "Who are you playing with?" And he said, "The boy," and of course my husband and I couldn't see the boy. And we asked, "What boy?" And he took a deep breath and kind of shrugged his shoulders, kind of hung his head, and turned around, he points and goes, "That one there." Like, why can't you see what's in front of you? He just couldn't believe that grandma and grandpa couldn't see this little boy playing with him.

This would continue. He'd always be playing with Jimmy—that's what Jacob said his name was.

Can Jacob still see Jimmy?

Jacob is going to be 12 next week, and he can't really see Jimmy like he used to. He remembers playing with Jimmy, he remembers the boy, he remembers doing things with him, but what he doesn't understand is why he can't see him like he used to. I think it's because he's gotten older. I think as we get older, I think we tend not to be able to see spirits because we're told they don't exist. His filters are in the way now, but he does remember playing with him and talking with him.

Tim Beauchamp
Grove, Oklahoma
December 1982

Tim Beauchamp was helping his mother at her horse farm when we spoke. We talked about baseball, horses, and ghosts. Tim's father was Jim Beauchamp, a major-league baseball player whose career spanned from 1963 to 1973. Beauchamp played for the St. Louis Cardinals, the New York Mets, and the Houston Astros, among other teams. Tim was born on opening day of the new Astrodome, and he says with pride that his father was the first to hit a homerun in the new arena, though it was a few days before opening day, so he's not sure if it's in the record books or not.

Today, Tim is 40 years old and works in technology, but he's been around farms and horses his entire life. When he was in high school, his parents divorced, remarried, and moved away. Young Tim wanted to finish high school in Grove with his friends, so he moved in with his grandparents at their farmhouse—a home where he experienced several peculiar happenings, but one supernatural event he remembers in great detail.

What was the farmhouse like?

It was the old family farm. My dad had been raised there, and it had been in the family for quite some time. The house had burned down when my father was young—his brother and sister were all in school at the time. It burned down around the time of the Depression. Money was pretty scarce. My grandfather was an attorney and he made pretty decent money, but back then in the Depression everybody was struggling, so they had to live in the garage until they rebuilt the house on the old foundation.

The rebuilt house was a much more solid structure made out of brick. They kept adding on to the house as times got better, and it became sort of a rambling ranch house.

Do you know when the original house was built?

No, I don't. That's all real vague to me. As far as the house being built on the foundation and all that, I received that information from my grandpa, and I really haven't researched or questioned it that much. I just took his word for it. But I do remember my dad telling me how hard it was to live in the garage while they were rebuilding the house.

What happened when you lived there?

First of all, I don't consider myself a medium, but I am one who has experienced more than my fair share of the paranormal. I do believe there are people who are mediums, and I think there might even be some on my mom's side of the family. I have had several ghost experiences and I'm one of those people that feel. I do think that I'm on the cusp of being a medium.

I believe everyone has a range of human senses, but there are some of us whose sensory experiences are a little bit outside that range. And I think some animals experience those ranges that most people do not see. And I think a lot of times you'll have dogs or something like that that will experience the same thing that some mediums might experience. I do feel I'm one of those people, especially regarding spirits and stuff. I have always felt like there was something—some kind of weight or some kind of sadness surrounding that property. Some times were worse than others, and sometimes I feel like maybe a spirit is stronger at certain times than others. I hadn't really broached the subject with my grandparents; I was kind of embarrassed about it. I mean, how do you talk about it? And there were some physical things about the house, too. I still remember it to this day—how certain spots in the house would just be ice cold. You could pass through it; it was really weird. I got the sense that I was being watched a lot, and I also heard footsteps. My bedroom was right next to the basement that had remained from the old house, and sometimes I could hear what I thought were footsteps coming up from the basement. It was really bizarre.

In 1982 I was in high school. I was watching TV and we were experiencing a snowstorm. It was extremely cold, and I started hearing this really bizarre noise. It sounded like a mewling sound—an animal or something. It sounded like an injured calf. In this area of Oklahoma, my mom has cattle and stuff, so that's not something that you wouldn't hear. But at the same time, I've never heard a calf make that kind of noise.

Would a calf ever be so close to the house that you could hear it inside?

No. It sounded very close. It sounded like it was right outside the window. The hair on the back of my neck went up. I kind of sensed that the noise was spiritual—my senses were just like, "Uh-oh…this is not right." I didn't want to go outside. I was scared to death. My grandparents were asleep, and I hated waking them up because my grandfather was really gruff. I was like, "Okay, I'm not going to wake them up, but I've got to find out what this is or I'll never get to sleep tonight." So I walked outside and started looking around and the snow was coming down. It wasn't quite a white-out or anything like that, it was just slowly snowing. I was scanning the horizon, and I heard the sound again and realized it was above me.

I just froze. I slowly looked up and there was a glowing ball of light in the tree. And it seemed like the noise was coming directly from that light. It made a mewling sound. I'll try to make the noise, it was like: [*he makes a noise that sounds like a cross between a young bleating sheep and a whining cat*]. Like that, sort of. As it made the sound, the light would grow brighter and then it would dim. I didn't know what to do. [*Laughs.*] It was like one of those dreams where you're so scared you can't talk or move. That's how I felt. Frozen in place for a while. And it was so cold, and that didn't help things either.

How far away from the light were you?

Not far. I was at the base of the tree, and it was about 20 feet (6 m) from me. It was like in the tree, but not on the tree. It was hovering over a branch. So I shuffled back into the house, and this time I didn't care how mad my grandfather got, I was waking him up. [*Laughs.*] I am not going to experience this by myself.

What time was it?

It was about 11:30 or midnight. I went in and I could barely speak. I was so scared, my voice was quivering. I was like, "Grrranndpaaa...." [*Laughs.*] And he woke up and said "What...what...what?" Again, he was really a gruff kinda guy. He was a small guy, but he was real gruff. He said, "What's the problem?" And I said, "There's a noise outside." And he said, "What do you mean there's a noise?" I said, "Well, there's a noise and there's something in the tree." And he said, "Well, what does it sound like?" And I mimicked the noise, and when I did that he turned pale and turned away.

He was not the kind of guy that would cry or anything like that, but he got teary-eyed and I could tell he was really upset. I asked him what was wrong and he said, "My little brother was born in the original farmhouse." He said his brother was born with a harelip and he had a cleft palate. He couldn't nurse and he died as a baby. Back then, there was nothing they could do for him. My grandpa said I made the exact noise that his brother made. He wanted to know where the sound was coming from, so I went out and pointed up in the tree and he said that would've been where the nursery was.

Did you know your grandpa had a brother?

I had never heard that story. I didn't know anything about my great uncle who had died. No one ever really talked about it—it was kind of a secret or something. After this happened, I mentioned it a couple of times and then I started hearing more and more about it. My mother told me that the baby was buried with my great-grandmother when she died. They put her tombstone right next to the baby's. They're buried about a mile or two (1.6 km to 3.2 km) away from the house in a cemetery.

Is the farmhouse still in your family?

My grandmother passed away, and then my grandfather sold it—I think it was back in the late 80s when he sold it. I'm not sure who owns it now. We used to be out there and were surrounded by pastures, but now the town of Grove has sort of moved out that way. They built a high school baseball field right across from the house called Jim Beauchamp Field, which is named after my dad.

What do you make of your encounter that night?

I could see my great uncle's spirit saying, "Look, here I am. The family won't even acknowledge me," you know, that kind of thing. It was kind of sad when I realized there's this great uncle I'd never heard about. He was almost forgotten because he died as a baby.

Kim Strain
Sitka, Alaska
1983

Kim Strain was born in picturesque southeast Alaska in a town called Wrangell. Her father worked as a safety consultant, so he traveled often and occasionally the family needed to relocate. When Kim was 11 years old, she and her family moved to Sitka, Alaska, another coastal town where they moved into their first house. The family was thrilled to have their own place, but according to Kim, they weren't alone in that house. Today she is a 38-year-old mom and certified nurse's assistant in Anchorage, Alaska.

What was the house in Sitka like?

It was our first house. It was a mill house—my father worked for the mill; he was a safety inspector there. The mill built these houses for all of the salaried workers, and that's what it was. It was just a three-bedroom, ranch style, and the house next to it looked just like it. I mean they were all exactly alike. But ours was a little different in that it had an add-on to the property so it was bigger. The property had a lot of mounds, and it was really very distorted. The property we were on was really weird compared to everybody else's—they were on flat property and we were on a hill.

When you moved in, did you get any strange sense of the place? Did you feel uncomfortable?

No, I didn't, actually. We were so excited when we first moved in because it was our first house—we'd always lived in apartments, and we knew that this was going to be for us. My sister and I were just excited about who got which room…no, I didn't have any strange feelings about the place. It probably took a few months of living there before I started having different sensations in the house that made me uncomfortable.

What kind of sensations?

I started having a feeling like I could hear somebody talking, but I couldn't actually tell where it was coming from. It sounded like somebody would be talking in another room, almost like a radio was on but it was on really low. I'd look around for where this radio was playing from, but it would never be there. The talking actually sounded like that, like a program was playing, not like somebody was talking at me, but like I was listening to some program or something. It was very strange.

My dad went away for this trip, and I got to sleep in his bedroom that night because he had the waterbed and my sister and I used to always fight over that, but I got the waterbed. He also had a TV in that room, and I was really excited about that. I remember sitting on the bed, leaning against the headboard, and I was eating popcorn.

I was watching the TV and I heard what sounded like something rustling behind the door to the bedroom. The bedroom door was open and it was against the wall—it sounded like something was behind there, like an animal. We had cats and dogs, so I thought maybe that's what the sound was, so I looked, and stopped chewing. I stopped to listen and look over there, but there was nothing back there, so I continued to watch my program and all of a sudden… even thinking about this just makes the hair stand up on my arms;

talking about it even now…I heard this voice in my ear. It said, "Excuse me, Kim." I know it's a weird thing to say…I don't know why those were the words, but that's what it said. It sounded like it was meant for me; it sounded like it was right in my ear, like somebody leaned right into my ear and spoke it.

Literally, I was paralyzed with fear. I could not move, my mouth went dry, and my heart started pounding—you know, that whole fight-or-flight syndrome. I just panicked. I didn't know what to do.

It was just a second later that it happened again—those same words. And that time I flew off that bed and raced into the living room—popcorn went flying, and I just stood there completely horrified. I mean I couldn't even…I was so scared…I was so scared. My mom was out there, and I told my mom about it. She said I was overreacting, of course. But I know what I heard, and I know it was in there. And when I think about what happened, at the moment that it happened, I could not hear any other sounds in the room. Almost like all of the other sounds in the area were gone and I was like in a…it's very hard to explain. It's like all of the sounds got sucked out of the room. That moment just stands out as being so intense. And everything in that room just seemed to be gone. Do you understand what I'm trying to say? That's what happened. Anyway, I refused to go back that night. Of course I went back later, but I would not even go back in there to turn the TV off or anything. My mom went in there and did that for me and cleaned up the popcorn and stuff. I did go on to have a couple other experiences in that house but not as intense as that.

What else happened?

It was around the same time; I'm going to say it was maybe even the same year or the next year, but it was after this first event. I was walking home, and it was just starting to get dark out. I come along this curve, and at this curve I can look up and see my house clearly from the road, and I could see the kitchen. If the kitchen light was on, I could usually see movement in the house and know who was home, or if my sister was in there or whatever. I'm walking along and I look up, and there's my mom standing in the window, and she's looking out at me. And the look on my mom's face—I'm going to call it my mom, because that's what it looked like to me—was like my mom, but an evil form or something. It was a very angry face, full of hatred, and it was looking right at me like it knew I was coming, like she knew I was there. But there's no way she could've known I was there. She was looking right at me, and I remember being horrified because she was so angry looking, and my mom doesn't look like this; she's just a really nice person. I thought I had done something really terrible or something; I couldn't think about what it was that would make her look like that.

So I came rushing closer to the house, looking at my mom the whole time. The face stayed that way, it seemed to turn as I walked, watching me the whole way. I came rushing into the house because I wanted to know what I had done, what was wrong. I come barging through the house and the lights were all on, which was normal for my family, but there was nobody in the house. I was calling for my mother, I thought she may have gone into the back room, but there was nobody home at all. I was so sure that my mom was standing there looking at me out that window that at that moment I became afraid because I knew that I'd seen something strange in the window.

What did you do next?

I called my mom. I called all around and found out that my parents were at some kind of work party or something. Anyway, I contacted my mom and was crying and asked for her to come home—and of course they wouldn't—and I ended up waiting outside for my family to come home.

Do you have any idea why this was happening there?

Honestly, I don't. I have no idea. I thought about it later. I can't imagine if it was maybe something that was in the house before us. The houses were built in the late 40s. And I don't know this for sure, this is all hearsay, but the people who lived there before us had a lot of problems. The kids were in and out of jail, that kind of thing. So there were some issues with the people in the house, like a lot of anger and stuff like that. I don't know if those things stay behind, I have no idea.

What did your mom say when you told her about seeing her figure in the window?

My mom truly believes that she is a psychic and that I happen to be able to see that kind of stuff, too. She doesn't know if it was a ghost or anything, but she thinks I can pick up vibrations.

Have you ever heard of a doppelganger?

Yes I have. It's the other form of the other person, or the other self. I never even thought of that. Later, when I talked to some people about this, someone told me that maybe I felt guilty about something, I tried to think about what I felt guilty about, but I couldn't think of anything. But I was a teenager, so it could've been a lot of things. [*Laughs.*] Maybe I felt guilty and it was my fears reflecting themselves on the window. I don't believe that. At the time it just didn't seem like that. I truly think that I saw something in that house.

How have things been for you since you moved out of the house?

I have never had an experience like that again. I've had feelings before, but never anything like that.

Has anyone else in your family experienced anything there?

My sister has experienced things in that house, and my children have experienced things in that house, but only a couple of them. And I have six kids. [*Laughs.*] Two of them have had experiences in the house. That home is still in our family and we rent it out. When I moved back to Sitka, I ended up living in the home almost five more years as an adult.

In that same room that it I heard the voice, my daughter, she's 14 now, used to refuse to sleep in that room because she believed that there was an owl—something she called an owl—living in the closet there. She said the owl used to stare at her from the closet, and this went on for like three years.

One time I sent my son back to the house when we were all at the park, which was near the house. I sent him to get something for a picnic or something, I can't remember, but he went to the house and the doors were locked, so he went around to go in through his window. He climbed halfway through the window, and he said he heard…and he swears to this day…that he heard people talking about him coming through the window in the house. He said he heard a bunch of people saying, "He's coming through the window, what are we going to do?" He came flying back to that park—he didn't come back with what I sent him for—he refused to complete his entry into the house. That's the only experience he ever had.

Janie Le'Kay
Birmingham, England
June to September 2003

Janie Le'Kay and her three children moved into a house in Birmingham, England, in June 2003 and signed on for a six-month lease. But the house didn't feel quite right to her. In some hauntings, it's the little things that add up over time. Perhaps a cold spot, some knocks, but sometimes things build. Janie, who was 29 years old at the time, and especially her young daughter, experienced many of these little peculiarities. But it was her mother who saw something more in the house while babysitting one evening. Janie moved out two months early from the end of her lease and lost the rent—something she didn't mind doing, because it meant getting away from the house.

When did you start feeling that something wasn't right with your home?

In May of 2003 we moved in. About a week into moving in, I just started to feel a little bit uneasy about the house. You know when you move to a property, or you're in the property, and you get a feeling about it? And it's either a really nice, warm, happy feeling, or it's a just not-quite-settled feeling? I just felt like it wasn't going to be my house.

When did you start to experience something?

My little girl, Fay, who was probably about 2 1/2 at the time, she was very unsettled in that house from about the first week that we moved in. She was not sleeping through the night at all. She was waking up crying all of the time. I had two other boys at the time, and they were very unsettled in there, too. They just weren't sleeping very well.

How old were the boys?

The boys...one was about 3 1/2 and the other was about 4 1/2. They're very young children and I've got all three of them in one room. The house was set so their bedroom was adjacent to mine, with the stairs between and no other rooms upstairs, just a staircase going up and a room at either side of the staircase. From that first week, we started to notice that it [*the house*] didn't have a nice feeling to it.

I started noticing things. The bathroom is actually downstairs in that house, so if I went down to the bathroom during the night, there was sort of a worried feeling. I was running through the kitchen into the bathroom and then quickly running back through the kitchen and upstairs to bed. I had a sort of the edgy feeling. This is ongoing.

My little girl was waking up going, "Someone is pinching my feet, mom! Someone is pinching my feet waking me up." She would wake up and start crying and shouting, "It's pinching, it's pinching!" I'd go in and say, "It's not pinching, sweetheart, your toes are cold, or you've just got a cramp in your foot." This was constant. She'd wake up during the night, like every other hour. She'd wake up and it was just really shattering and horrendous.

How did the boys sleep?

The boys slept a little better than that, though they did get awoken quite a lot in that particular house. This just went on and on. I wasn't actually there very long because we were unsettled in there; we wanted to move out.

Fay had it the worst. I used to go and settle her. I'd probably get her a drink and take her down to the toilet, and get her back into bed. Every time I would go through to the room, I started thinking, "Oh God, was that something on the stairs?" [*Laughs.*] Because the stairs were very dark between the two rooms, and there was a wall on each side of the stairs, so they were enclosed with a door at the bottom. We used to shut the bottom door, that led into the kitchen, so those stairs were very, very dark as you were going between the rooms, and sometimes I felt I could see something at the bottom of the stairs. I'd say, "Oh, for God's sake, don't be silly. It's the middle of the night, you're tired, you're half-asleep walking through to the bedroom. You probably just caught whatever in the corner of your eye." But it was really bothering me.

I noticed that a few times I'd walk past the stairs and I kind of thought, "Oh, I saw something there." Or the door at the bottom of the stairs would be open, and it's usually closed—'cause it has a little latch on it and I would latch it because I wanted us to be locked up, do you know what I mean? So I'd unlock that bottom door and then run to the kitchen and lock it again on the way up. And sometimes the door would actually be open, which puzzled me. This was going on and on.

I had a six-month lease on the house. This was sort of ongoing for the first few months. Then one evening my mother was baby-sitting the children overnight, and me and my partner had gone to a wedding. I said to Mom, "Fay's going to be waking up most of the evening, but you just have to run upstairs to her. And my mom said, "I'll sleep on the couch and watch telly. I'll stay awake and listen out for her."

My mom is as straightlaced as they get—she would never tell lies. She kept getting woken up by Fay. "Nanny, it's pinching my toes, pinching my toes." My mom would go in and comfort her, get her a drink, and settle her back off to sleep. Fay was really unsettled that night. It got to the point where my mom said, "I'm not going to keep running up and down the stairs to go and see Fay." So she went and laid on our bed, which was in the other room adjacent. So at least then she just had to go between the rooms.

My mom had sort of dozed off in the bedroom and suddenly,

apparently she heard this really loud rumbling coming up the stairs. She was like, "What is that?" She said it sounded like people running up the stairs. If it had been me, I would have thought it was my little boys who had gone running up and down the stairs.

Mom wondered what it was and she rubbed her eyes, and at the bottom of the bed there were three people—it was two men and a lady. My mom was absolutely panic-stricken. The first thing she said was, "What do you want?" And they said, "We've come for my glass bowl."

She said, "This is my daughter's house and my daughter is not here. You have to come back another time." It was the first thing she thought of saying. It wasn't like, "Call the police, there's people in the house." She said they just kind of stood there. She said they looked solid, they didn't look wispy or anything. The first thing she thought was to tell them they've got to come back, this isn't her house, and, "You're going to wake the children."

She said they didn't argue, but just sort of turned around and glided out of the room. There was no sound to them going back down the stairs. And she sat there utterly terrified, crying by now because she was so panicked. She knew that it wasn't something natural because there was no noise; they just kind of drifted out of the bedroom. She said at first she thought it was like a dream, because they were so solid. She thought there were actually people there. But she said there's no way it was a dream because she'd stayed awake and sat on the bed sort of shaking.

She managed to pluck up the courage to go down the stairs and check the house out. She went down the stairs, and she phoned my dad and he came round immediately. I think he stayed with her the rest of the night, if I recall.

She's just so straightlaced; it's the last thing she'd ever come out with. And she didn't actually tell me about this until the day I was moving out. This happened to her about a month or two before we moved out. My partner already had a house, and he would stay with me regularly at my house with the children. I then decided to move out of the house and into his house because his lodgers had moved out. On the morning that we started shifting the stuff out, mom said to me, "Right, you're not staying in this house overnight again, are you?" And I said, "No." And she said, "And you're definitely not going to be in here on your own at night or really anytime?" And I said, "No. Why?"

I'd arranged to move out before my lease had finished because I didn't want to stay there any longer. I didn't feel nice there. So I said to my mom, "We're definitely moving out today." We had the vans, collected all of the stuff, so she knew I wasn't staying there. And then she told me what had happened. And I was horrified. I said, "Oh my God, you let me stay in this house?" She said, "I didn't want to tell you before because I knew you'd have to sleep there and you wouldn't be happy about sleeping here knowing that something like that had happened."

What really spooked us, and my mom didn't actually know about this, but when we moved into the house, it was completely empty. It wasn't furnished. The only thing that was in the house was a big, old, glass bowl which was on the side of the kitchen. And my mom didn't know that. And that is what this woman had asked for. These visitors had come to collect it. And when I told her that, that of course made her blood run cold. Because she was trying to convince herself it was a dream. And it wasn't.

Did you leave the bowl when you moved out?

Oh God, yeah. [*Laughs.*] We used it for fruit and stuff like that, but it was always kept carefully away from the children's reach. I always made sure that the bowl had been kept nicely. And when we left, I gave it a clean and I put it exactly where it had been.

I spoke to the landlord as I was moving out. He said, "How come you're moving out early?" And I told him I never felt really settled in the house, and I said, "Has anyone ever mentioned anything strange about the house?" And he said, "No." And I said, "That bowl that was in the kitchen...." He said, "Yeah?" I said, "Is that yours? Did you buy it when you bought the house?" And he said, "No, that bowl's always been in there. It was the previous owner's."

I said, "Do you mind if I ask some more questions?" And he said, "No, why?" And I said, "Well, we had some really strange experiences in this house. Just little things, nothing major. It's just that my little girl was very unsettled in the house. And I'd see the occasional thing out of the corner of my eye." I asked who lived in the house before, and he said it was an elderly lady and her two grown-up sons—which were the people that my mom had seen. Now the sons, as far as we know, were still alive. They'd moved far away from the area after their mother had died. They sold the house to the landlord, and they moved out. So it was those three people from his description of the sons—they were the people that my mom had seen with this lady who had come back to get this glass bowl.

There's not really much sense as far as the pinching of toes. We don't know what was going on there, but that stopped as soon as we moved out. Fay never woke up again at night; they all slept through lovely. I always felt that children are more open to things.

I was so thankful my mom hadn't told me about this before, because I couldn't have spent another night there.

Sharon Moritz
Chicago, Illinois
1966

Once in a while, people encounter a specter that they recognize. Though the ghost doesn't resemble anyone they knew in life, nevertheless, the figure is known. The Angel of Death is often depicted as a dark figure in a black cloak, and that's exactly what Sharon Moritz saw in the home she was living in back in 1966. Sharon instantly feared the worst for her infant daughter. Today, the 57-year-old factory worker lives in Lindenhurst, Illinois, but she has never forgotten the haunted house she lived in nor the dark figure she saw there.

What was your life like back in 1966?

I was married and I had a baby. She was born in April of '66, and at the time we were living with my in-laws because we had had a fire in our apartment. We had to have a place to live right away, so we were living there for a few months. So much stuff has gone on in that house it's just incredible.

What kinds of things?

I guess there were a lot of tragedies that happened at that house. My sister-in-law, she was about 16 at the time, her boyfriend came in and shot and killed himself in the basement. And then when I had gotten divorced, maybe around 1968, later on my husband was bipolar and he murdered his father in the kitchen.

When they first moved into the house, in this one bedroom there was a rotten smell. They couldn't get rid of it. They tore the wallpaper down, they redid the floors, they redid everything, and they just couldn't get rid of this rotten stink—like a dead body, you know that kind of smell? And then my husband's aunt, she also lived there with them, she was very in-tune to parapsychology and this type of stuff. They had a priest come in a couple of times and bless the room, but that didn't work. She had some kind of mixture of incense or something like that that she started to burn, and then eventually the smell went away, but it was there for very long time. That was all before 1966.

Did you get a creepy feeling living in that house?

Oh my God…it was horrible. [*Laughs.*] I never wanted to be upstairs alone. When we first got married, I was very young and I got pregnant, you know, so you have no money. We just lived there for a couple of months, and I was terrified to stay upstairs by myself. There was an attic, and in the front of the house was a bedroom, and in the back of the house was a bedroom. We were in the back bedroom.

My husband would go to work in the morning, and I would take the two dogs upstairs with me. During one particular incident, I was lying in bed, and all of a sudden something grabbed my hair from behind—because the bed wasn't up against the wall… and the light, you know the hanging light? It started spinning and spinning and spinning.

I was just frozen. I was so scared, and you know how you open your mouth and nothing comes out? And my mother-in-law, she was downstairs and she said that she got a funny feeling, she thought something was wrong so she came to the bottom of the stairs and started calling me. She wanted to make sure I was okay, and then everything stopped. So I flew downstairs, and from then on I wouldn't go upstairs alone unless I had the dogs with me.

We didn't stay in the house much longer, and we got our own apartment. Everywhere in that house it was creepy. You'd be downstairs in the evening watching TV and you'd hear somebody walking around up there. We go up there to see who it was, and nobody was there.

What event stood out the most there?

This particular incident, my husband had gone to work and the baby was upstairs. We were in the front bedroom this time and she was asleep in her crib. I left the bedroom door open and the attic door open so I would hear her, and I just laid on the couch after my husband had left.

Were you in the attic?

No. From the dining room there was a door that opened—that's what we called the attic door, and then you go up the staircase and you're in the attic. To your left was the back bedroom, and you had to walk through the attic and then there was the other bedroom. So we had two open doors so I could hear her.

It was, like, five or six o'clock in the morning. My father-in-law, he was a fireman, so he was gone for 24 hours at a time. So I was just lying there on the couch and I fell asleep and something woke me up. I didn't know what it was, but it startled me and I opened my eyes. I looked and I saw this hooded figure, this person in this robe with a hood up, walking through the dining room and then around the dining room table to the open door, and it disappeared. It went in there and then it started up the stairs.

I was like, "Oh my God." I jumped up and I started running. Right off the dining room was my mother-in-law's bedroom and I yelled into there, "Mamma, get up quick!" I don't know exactly what it was, but I wanted her to get up. I ran up the stairs and into the bedroom and the baby was just laying there...her eyes were rolling in her head and she was limp.

So I grabbed her and I ran downstairs to my mother-in-law and said, "Look, look! Help me, help me, something's wrong." She's trying to revive the baby and everything and she told me run to the store, which was just a few doors down on the corner, she says run down there and get a 7UP. So I ran to the store, got a 7UP, ran back, and she's getting the 7UP into the baby.

In the meantime she had called a taxi and we were taking the baby to a doctor. I don't remember if she called ahead or what... I don't remember exactly, but by the time we got to the doctor, the baby was fine. Absolutely fine. The doctor said, "There's absolutely nothing wrong with her." The doctor was like, well, you guys are nuts.

What do you think the dark figure was?

I don't know if this thing was going to get her, or if it was warning me. I don't really know what the whole story behind it could've been.

It's been a long time since this happened. Do you have any thoughts now?

Sometimes I think that it was like the Angel of Death. But I think if it were him, why would he wake me? Why would I see this happening? Or something else woke me letting me know that I have to save my daughter. It could've been something else that woke me to see this and then I ran up there and got her in time. The figure wasn't glowing or anything; it was a dark hooded figure. It wasn't a good thing, I don't think. I'm thinking maybe that's what it was—he came to get my daughter.

Once you ran up the stairs, did you see it again?

No, there was nothing up there. Nothing up there at all.

Is your daughter okay today?

Yeah, she's fine today. I figure she was probably 7, maybe 8 months old at the time so she doesn't remember any of it.

Did anything else peculiar happen around the baby in that house?

There was another incident when my husband was working nights. I would wake up because you know, the baby would wake up crying because she wants a bottle or whatever...you know how they do that. She would start crying, and I would lie in bed and think, Oh God, I'm so tired. I don't want to get up, maybe she'll go back to sleep. One night I heard somebody come in from the attic, and I thought maybe it was my mother-in-law, but there was nobody there. But the footsteps kept coming and it would go over by the crib, and the baby shut up and went back to sleep.

I told my husband, "This is what's happening, I want to get out of here, there's too much going on in this house. I've gotta get out of here." He'd say, "Ahh, you're just dreaming," or whatever. So one night he was there and I told him, "When this happens, I'm going to wake you up so you can experience this"—because it started happening on a nightly basis. The baby woke up, she started crying, and I stayed there and waited and then I heard it. So I started waking my husband up. I said, "Come on, come on, wake up, here it comes...."

So now the two of us are underneath the covers. I knew whatever it was wasn't going to harm her; it was comforting her. So this particular night that I woke him up to experience this, the door opened and the footsteps walked over to the baby and they were there for awhile, and she went to sleep, and the footsteps left. I had never heard them leave before. The footsteps left and the door closed. And he says, "That's it, we're outta here."

After moving out, did you ever experience anything like that again?

No, not at that level. I'll never forget it. My aunt, she swears that what happened to my ex-husband…killing his father in that house…something from the house did that to him, to make him. My aunt is dead now, but she swore up and down that that's what it was. It took over him, something in the house.

Morris Sabanski
Toronto, Ontario, Canada
Late 1950s to mid-1970s

Morris Sabanski is a man of science. He has three degrees: two in chemistry, and one in engineering. The 55-year-old has lectured at the university level, and he was a management consultant before retiring. He now lives in Australia, where he enjoys feeding the wild king parrots and kookaburras that come to his deck for food.

Morris has a unique perspective on ghosts, or "spooks" as he calls them. He grew up in a very active haunted home in Toronto where years of unexplained experiences made him question some of the science he was learning as he got older. His questions led to more questions, as they often do, and he's intrigued by some of the theories that quantum physics may offer in explaining some supernatural phenomena.

It's the kind of thing that can't be dismissed that easily. There are people who walk around saying, "I saw a shining light and it was really my dead grandmother waving to me," or, "I had this funny feeling…." All of those kinds of stories, whether or not the person who experienced them really did is not the issue, but whatever they experienced can quite often be explained as relatively conventional phenomena. That kind of stuff we had all the time back in Toronto. So many of these things are pretty much ho-hum. I've had so much experience with these things over my lifetime, I effectively grew up with this stuff.

Can we start in your house in Toronto back in the 1970s?

The house we grew up in was a pretty conventional house—a pretty normal, cookie-cutter kind of house built in the normal track of the type of houses that sprung up during the 50s or thereabouts. The house was perfectly nondescript, one of maybe 50 or 60 houses in this one little enclave. We moved into the house in the late 1950s or thereabouts—I'm kind of vague on dates, but the generality of what I'm going to tell you is reasonably accurate. The house had a basement, a ground floor, and an upper story. The upper story contained three bedrooms and a bathroom, the ground floor contained a rather large living room and the kitchen towards the back of the house, and also to one side of the house was access to the basement. With the basement you go downstairs and that encompasses the entire perimeter of the house. The house faced the street, there was a garden to the front of the house, and there was a long gravel driveway that came up from the road alongside of the garden up to the side of the house.

If you've never been to Toronto, about eight months of the year it's bloody cold. You've got snow on the ground probably six months of the year. So for probably three or four months of the year, the driveway was clear, the gravel was loose, and it served the function that if anybody walked up the driveway, you could hear them. We used it as a kind of warning system. We'd hear somebody walking up the driveway, would look out the window, and sure enough, most of the time, it was somebody walking up the driveway come to visit. But some of the time we'd look out the window and there'd be nobody there. After a while, we came to realize that this noise is giving us some indication of spooks as well.

Very soon after we moved in, we started to experience the phenomenon of the doors opening and closing by themselves, which at first we thought was the house settling or whatever, despite the fact that the house had been there for a long time. We said, "Ah, it's the house settling, wind," you know, all the usual conventional explanations, except for the fact that the doors would lock. They would lock—as in the latch would catch—to the extent that you had to turn the knob in order to open the door. But nevertheless, the doors would open and close, the lights would go on and off, and there were footsteps going up and down the stairs and walking around the top floor, particularly around the bedroom area and the landing area at the top of the stairs. All these kinds of things started shortly after we moved in, and after a period of time it became evident to us that these were common occurrences and we more or less got used to them.

We had one bathroom on the second floor. As a family, we had a mother, a father, and five kids. [*There were*] four sisters and me—I was in the middle. So we all got up around the same time when we had to go to school, or to work, or whatever the case. As you would expect, it was like a sorority house; there was a big rush for the bathroom. Well, quite often it was the case that we're all standing outside the bathroom twiddling our thumbs, and there's somebody in there. Okay, the door's locked, we can hear water splashing around inside, we can hear movement inside, all the kinds of things and noises associated with doing one's morning thing in there. The trouble is we looked around, there's Mom, there's Dad, there's five kids standing around outside the door. And we'd say, "Well, who is in the bathroom?" This would go on probably five, 10 minutes, the noises would stop, the bathroom door would open by itself, and there's nobody there. But there's water splashed around the sink, there's water on the floor, the towels are wet, all this kind of stuff. So after a while we got to realize that, okay, we've got spook number one living in here.

And using the bathroom.

Yeah. We also quickly drew the association with the lights coming on, the footsteps, all that kind of stuff. We figured out we've got a spook living in here, and these are the manifestations of this person, he/she, or whatever. So that was number one.

Some years later, we discovered that this spook number one was an old man who lived there, and he obviously hadn't figured out the fact that he was dead and was supposed to be doing something else. So he was continuing with his conventional life.

The number two spook was the one that we considered to be bloody dangerous. We figured out that he was probably an ex-Jesuit priest because of his behavior, because of the historical location the house was built on, and because of the way we saw him when he appeared.

I talked to a guy who was a member of a local historical society some years after I had left home, and I said, "What's the history of the area?" One thing led to another, and he told me that somewhere in the area of this housing tract, some 100s of years before, there had been a Jesuit mission. This Jesuit mission had been ultimately attacked by the local Indians who figured they'd had enough of these bloody Jesuits. They'd gone in there and slaughtered them all and burned down the mission. It was never rebuilt, so nobody knows exactly what the location of this was. But by process of deduction, since it's the only area that you can make any substantial structure is where this housing tract is, the general assumption is that this is where the mission was built.

Okay, this has relevance with this second, dangerous spook. We had family pets; we had dogs and cats. The dog was a German Shepherd—this was at the time when really imaginative people named her "Doggie." Her usual practice was at night when we all went to bed or were going to bed, she'd come up to the second story and she would sleep in the corridor adjacent to the bedrooms halfway between the landing for the steps and the front of the house. It was quite frequent where she'd be fast asleep, then all of a sudden she'd wake up. She'd stand in the middle of the room, the hair on her back standing straight up, you know. The hackles were up, her teeth were bared, and she could see something that we can't see. She's growling and barking and making a general ruckus, and we would stand there and we couldn't see anything, we couldn't feel anything, but it was quite obvious that she was responding to something. This would go on sometimes for a minute or two and she'd settle down and go back to sleep. So that brought our attention to the fact that there was something else going on here.

Now in addition to that, we start to develop a rather interesting thing. My sisters in particular had this thing where they'd sometimes arrive home and absolutely refuse to go into the house. They'd be terrified to go in the front door. It could be 40 below zero and they would be sitting on the front steps. There's obviously something there. There was something about the house that they were just absolutely terrified to go inside. I would come home from wherever I'd be and I'd see them sitting there freezing on the front steps, and I'd say, "Oh, okay, so the spook's back again." Then I go and check the door. It didn't bother me at all, so we go inside and whatever was there was gone and we'd go about our normal business. But that particular aspect influenced my sisters a lot more than it did me. There was only one occasion in my life when I experienced anything similar.

After I had grown up and moved out of the house, every so often my mother would go out of town for weeks on end and I'd look after the house. On this one particular occasion that I went over there, I think it was a Friday night and I figured I was going to stay for the weekend because the house needed some maintenance. So I arrived and I figured I've got to go down to the basement to get some equipment, some tools and things, and I'll get started working, right? So I go to the basement, I open the basement door, I'm about to go to the basement and I say, "There's no bloody way I'm gonna go down there." I was absolutely terrified. I spent 8 years in the service and I've had a rather interesting life, and there's really very little that scares me. But this absolutely and totally terrified me. There was no way I was going to go into the basement.

So I backed out, closed the basement door, and went away. A couple of hours later I figure, well, you know, let's try this again. Despite that it scared me, I'm going to check this out again. I open the basement door and there was nothing. I turn on the light, nothing. Went down the stairs, nothing. I wandered around the basement, I checked it all out, didn't see anything, didn't feel anything. I picked up the tools and things I needed, went up and went about my business. That feeling is what my sisters used to feel quite regularly when they'd wait by the front door. That's the first time that I personally experienced it, and I'll tell you, it scared me.

The reason we finally came to the conclusion that this was a Jesuit was because my sisters frequently said they woke up in the middle of the night, and they could see somebody standing at the foot of the bed and they described it. I said, "Yeah, yeah, yeah, fine." You know, I was kind of skeptical about this, but given everything else that happened I said, "Okay, it's possible, but I personally haven't seen it."

On one occasion, I stayed over at my mother's place because she was gone. I slept in the master bedroom upstairs, which I think was most convenient at the time. So here I was lying in bed fast asleep and I feel something pulling on my foot. You know how you are when you're fast asleep—you feel something, you kind of don't really wake up, you kind of go into a half-awakened state? So that happened. I go into this half-awakened state, something's pulling my foot, and I'm saying, "Ahhh…go away, I'm trying to sleep." I'm trying to sleep, but eventually it keeps persisting. It persists, it persists, and I finally wake up.

Now, on the left-hand side of the room is a large picture window which is open to the street, and I left the curtains open so the room was quite well-lit from the street lighting. So this thing is pulling my foot and pulling my foot, and finally I come to full consciousness. I wake up, I open my eyes, and I'm lying flat on my back staring at the ceiling. I sit up and right at the end of my bed I see this person standing there. Standing at the end of the bed is a guy wearing a hat, a big broad-brimmed hat and what's evidently a cape dropping down from the shoulders in kind of an A-shape. And all I can see is the silhouette—I can't see any features, I can't see anything at all. I can see this black form standing there—absolutely jet black, so there's no doubt at all that it's there.

So I wake up and look at this…whatever it is, and it presumably is looking back at me. I don't say anything and it doesn't say anything. I'm sitting there in bed perfectly wide awake, there's no doubt at all that I'm awake, and I'm looking at this entity, or whatever it is, and after a couple of minutes it starts to fade. I can start seeing through it. It fades, it becomes transparent, and finally it just kind of fades away and disappears. Over a period of a couple of minutes that happens.

That confirmed what my sisters had claimed that they had seen in the past. I spoke to them after this incident—none of us were living at home then, but we eventually got together and talked about it—and, yup, I described what they'd seen. We came to the conclusion, given the form that we could see and the dress, and given the history, this was the spook of a dead Jesuit. I'm making presumptions here, but we came to that conclusion.

So we concluded that the house was haunted by two entities; one is this old guy who's just going about his business, and the other was this Jesuit. It turned out that this Jesuit was a lot more than just a nuisance—he was bloody dangerous.

Do you think he could have hurt someone?

He could and did. We came to know when this particular entity or whatever it was was around because of the way the dog reacted. We drew the conclusion that when the dog had her hackles up and would suddenly jump up and run to the door and demand to be let out, it was time to be careful. We decided it was time to be careful because there was one occasion when this entity was around and it pushed my sister down the stairs.

She was hurt. She was standing at the top of the stairs, and she was just about to walk down when she was pushed from behind. It wasn't just one of those gentle little nudges; it was a very solid push, and she went flying through the air and she landed on the bottom stair. You can imagine a normal staircase; the vertical drop is about, what, 10 feet (3 m)? The horizontal is probably about the same, so she flew through the air, landed on the bottom stair, and broke her arm and had various other cuts and bruises and all the things you would expect from that kind of fall.

There's no doubt at all that she was pushed and it wasn't just an accidental little nudge. it was a deliberate push. Given that we knew that the entity was around at the time and that our dog demanded to go outside a couple of minutes before, we figured, okay, this guy's here, it's time to be really careful. This entity was just plain bloody evil. We learned to be careful with this guy, and when we knew that he was around, we would behave ourselves accordingly. If we were near the staircase, we made sure that we held onto the handrail. We didn't hang around at the landing and those kind of things. So we adjusted our lives accordingly which is probably a pretty smart thing because once you've been pushed down the stairs, you tend to remember that.

How often was phenomena occurring?

It was pretty much a daily occurrence. Something would happen, doors open and close, lights would go on and off, taps would turn on and off, electrical appliances would go on and off, and that kind of thing. That was pretty normal, we just took that as background noise, but the incident with footsteps in the rug was something that can't be dismissed.

What happened with the footsteps in the rug?

Let me start at the beginning. This was one of those occasions when my mother was away and I was looking after the house. So on the way home, I figured I'd drop in there and just look the place over and see if anything needed to be done. It was late at night, probably around 9:30 or 10 o'clock that I arrived. I went inside and I checked the house. Everything looked perfectly fine, no problems, so I figured, well, it's kind of late, I might as well watch the news, and I sat down in the living room. The room was a large rectangular room; it's probably twice as long as it is wide. So I sit down in the armchair in front of the TV set. I turn on the TV and start watching the news. I'm now facing more or less towards the front of the house and about 10 feet (3 m) away is this folding door. I'm watching TV, and the news comes on, and I hear the door rattle.

The rug on the floor is an elderly rug. It's been there since we lived in the house. It started out as a deep-pile rug, and over the years, with all of the traffic, people walking back and forth, and all that, as the rug has aged and the nap gets crushed down. So the nap is now crushed down pretty solidly. The folding door, in order for it to open has to be pulled, and it has to slide over this rug. Because of the thickness of the rug, despite the fact it's been tripped down with many years of use, there's still a fair bit of nap there and it's still hard to pull the sliding door over it. You can open and close it, but it requires some force.

So here I am sitting in the chair watching TV. To the left is the folding door which is closed, and I hear the folding door rattle. I look over, it's no big deal, I figured it was a bit of a breeze—I really don't think much of it. I go back to watching TV. A couple of minutes later I hear a rattle again, and this time I look and I'm sitting there watching the door open itself, go up against the wall, stay open for about 10 seconds, and then close again.

This requires a considerable amount of force to open. It's not something that house movement or a breeze or whatever is going to cause to happen. It's just not going to happen by itself, so something has caused this and obviously there's nobody standing there. But something has applied considerable force to this door to open and close it. I'm pretty impressed by this. Okay, this is a new one. It's something that you can't explain, you can't explain it with the house settling, you can't explain it by a breeze blowing through the house, you can't explain it by an earthquake, or anything like that.

A couple of weeks later, my mother has come back and I get a phone call from her. She says, "Come on over here and take a look at this." I said, "Now what's happened?" She said, "No, no, no...come on over, come on over." I said, "Okay."

So I hop in the car and drove over there. I said, "Okay, what's the story?" She says, "Come into the living room. Come in here." I said, "Okay, what?" And she points in the living room and I look down at the rug, and there's a set of footprints going from the folding door diagonally across the room to the center of the far wall.

Okay, fine, footprints in themselves are one thing, but recall what I said about this rug. It used to be a thick carpet which has now been crushed down except for the fact that the where the footprints are, the nap is standing straight up vertically as in a brand-new rug. So you've got very high contrast footprints going across the room from the folding doors to the wall in the opposite corner. They were very distinct footprints in that one of them was a boot. You know what a calvary boot looks like? It's got a heel and it's got kind of a square toe. There's one of those going across the room, and the other one is barefoot with five distinct toes, with a pad of the foot, with the arch, and the heel—very distinct. This lasted some months. We had various people come and visit, of course, and everybody saw it. Many, many people have seen it, and it took some months before normal traffic could obliterate these footprints.

If I could figure out how to make an old rug rejuvenate itself like that, I would be filthy rich in the carpet restoration business. It was one of those things that you couldn't explain by conventional phenomena. It's one of those things you can't just explain by imagination, or a trick of the eye, or whatever. This is something distinct, it's physical, and there's no doubt at all that it's there. It's standing right there for you.

Having been in a life of science, what do you make of these experiences?

If it hadn't been for the experiences that I had growing up in that house in Toronto, which exposed me to a somewhat different view of the world, I probably wouldn't be thinking what I'm thinking now, and I probably wouldn't be having the discussion that you and I are having now because I would've been locked into the conventional scientific thinking. This is the current dogma, this is what we believe, this is the way it is, and that's it: case closed. But when you've experienced A, B, [and] C, which is completely contrary to what conventional science tells you, all that tells you two things. One thing is that you start questioning conventional science, and two, you start questioning the people purporting conventional science. You say, "Okay what I've seen, they're saying doesn't exist, but clearly it does and what is it about all these other things over here on the right-hand side in science that I can question as well? Then you start hitting on a broader base of knowledge, such as when I studied quantum physics. The light starts coming on. The light only came on because I had the experience of growing up in that house.

I'm not sure whether I'm a believer or what. All I can say is I've experienced a number of phenomena, I have seen a number of things. I don't know what those things mean, I don't know what those things were. They could be a psychological aberration on my part, I accept that. But if someone can show me that, fine, I'll accept that. But at the moment, I'm at a point where I can say, I've seen this, I've experienced this, I don't know what it is, I have no explanation for it, but I can start speculating. And given my frame of mind and background, when I start speculating on what I have seen, then I go into the area of quantum physics.

Morris Sabanski's mother sold the house in 1995. He doesn't know if the people living there now have experienced anything like what his family experienced.

Chapter 2

Ghosts We Know

Photo credit: © istockphoto.com/Duncan Walker

There are a lot of natural phenomena that often get labeled as ghostly. For example, a flash of lightning may reflect off of a mirror and cast a strange specter on the wall for a second or two. Or someone may see a living person walk by the window of an abandoned building and believe this trespasser to be a ghost haunting the property. But when we encounter a ghostly image of someone we recognize—someone who we know has already passed on—the experience is among the most profound of all ghost encounters.

Oftentimes there are important messages to be delivered from the dead to the living. Though significant, these messages are often simple and speak of love, forgiveness, or maybe one last goodbye. The experience is one to be cherished by those who go through it.

Rev. Father Scott E. Kingsbury
Los Angeles, California
1966

Rev. Father Scott E. Kingsbury is a 48-year-old Anglican priest who lives in Los Angeles, California. I knew he was a nonorthodox priest for two very simple reasons. First, he wrote to me and said he believes in ghosts; and second, he was willing to talk about it on the record. I was intrigued as to how he fit the experience into his religion and faith. Father Kingsbury believes in ghosts because of an experience he had when he was 9 years old—an encounter that frightened him at the time, but an experience he's come to cherish.

Tell me about your upbringing.

My family history is actually kind of interesting. I am an only son, my father was an only son, his father's father was an only son, and my great-grandfather was an only son. I hate to say that my family tree doesn't fork—that has a different connotation—but we have a straight line of single male sons from as far back as I know my family history. I was sort of the crown prince of my family, as only sons are. Spoiled rotten. And one of my favorite things in life was to go spend time with Grandpa and Grandma, or as I called her, Nana. They were my paternal grandparents.

I believe this was end of the year—it may have been a winter break, I don't really recall—but I was going to go spend a week at Grandma and Grandpa's house. They lived not too far away over in the Beverly Hills area. As she always did, Grandma would come to pick me up. Grandpa didn't drive because he was blind—he had glaucoma—so Grandma would come. And you know what? He was probably a better driver than she was because this woman could not drive. She picked me up in her little Corvair, and she drove us over to her house over on the other side of L.A. She pulled up and I ran out of the car and ran into the house to go see my Grandpa, and I found him, as we say, dead as a doornail on the floor.

It was really tough because I had never dealt with death with anybody, and especially not my favorite person in the whole world, my Grandpa. It shocked me. Also the way he died was a little shocking. People die in all sorts of ways; you learn this in ministry, and through life. Grandpa died in the bathroom, facedown on the floor. I'd never seen anybody that color. It was quite a shock. And to the best of my knowledge, I had never screamed in my entire life until that moment. The only thing that came out was a bloodcurdling scream. I ran out and got my Grandma. She came in and called the fire department. In those days, there were no paramedics. You called the fire department. So the fire department came out.

I was standing there with the fire department, not wanting to go back inside, and a lady came from across the street and put her arm around me and said, "He's not dead, it's just an illusion." This was my first experience with a Christian Scientist. This confused my little 9-year-old head. I just saw him there with his pants around his knees, bright purple, laying on the floor, and this fire department guy told me he's dead and you're telling me he's not? Now I'm confused. I was disquieted.

After my Grandpa's funeral, and about five or six months later, I'm laying in my bed at my house. I was very used to, at that time, my father entering my bedroom to get socks or underwear out of drawers that were in my room. So hearing footsteps or feeling a presence was never shocking at predawn hours. But this night I woke bolt upright, and I don't know why, I didn't feel anything, no cold sensation, no nothing. I just looked up, and standing at the end of the bed was who I assumed was my father.

He was young, vibrant, and kind of glowing a little bit with a very benevolent look on his face, a very soft smile looking down on me and my bed. I said, "What are you doing here? It's too dark for you to be in here this early." And without words, [meaning telepathically] this person said to me the following things: "I'm so sorry that you found me." And at that moment it hit me that this isn't my dad, this is a younger, more vibrant, healthy version of my grandfather who, by the way, my dad looked like, and I'm starting to look like. If I wear my reading glasses and catch a glimpse of myself in the mirror, I go, "Dad?!" So the first thing he says is, "I'm sorry you found me." And then I got the 9-year-old chills. Goosebumps. I was frightened at that moment.

The second thing he said is, "I'm in a wonderful place and everybody's here." I still find that one of the most interesting things about this. "I'm in a wonderful place and everybody's here." I didn't ask if anybody was there; it wasn't the question that was on my mind.

And the third thing he said is, "You keep saying your prayers like I taught you. God's got something really special for you." And then he just disappeared. And I don't mean with a pop; he just sort of faded away like if you turn an old black-and-white TV off. And now I was scared. I got up, I turned on my light, I looked around, there's nothing there, and I went and I did something very strange—I hid in the bathtub. I pulled the curtain and then I decided that wasn't good because I had seen *Psycho*. So I went back to bed and I told nobody about this except for my mother, who just told me it was a dream.

What do you think your Grandpa's message meant?

Fast-forward many years. After my father and mother had died, I was cleaning up the last remnants of a group of boxes that had honestly never been opened since my Grandpa died. When you're the only son of an only son of an only son, you inherit all of the junk. So there was a box, and I opened this final box of all of the boxes, and I find at the bottom, my Grandpa and my Nana Kingsbury's marriage certificate. It was signed by Father Neil Dodd who founded St. Mary of the Angels, the parish I was at for 13 years. My grandparents were married at St. Mary of the Angels in Hollywood and I never knew it. That's where I was ordained, and that's where I served for 13 years. And it dawned on me, at that moment this crystal-clear thought came in my head, I said, "Oh my God, this is what Grandpa meant, that God's got something really special for me. That I'd be at St. Mary's and we would complete the circle." I don't tell this story often. My wife has heard the story and certain close friends, but very few people in the parish have I told. And I wouldn't talk about this from the pulpit.

Why not?

There's sort of a misunderstanding of the veil between life and death. In the Anglican Church there is something called the *via media*, which is Latin for "the middle way." It's halfway between Protestantism and Catholicism. There are those of us who lean way to the Catholic side, like me, and there are those who would lean way to the puritanical side, like people I don't know but I've read about. [*Laughs.*] But we get them all in the traditional Anglican Church, and I don't want to offend those more Protestant-leaning people who take the Bible literally, and who have a misunderstanding about Catholicism's idea about our belief in the communion of Saints. St. Paul says that neither height, nor depth, nor width, nor breadth, nor death, will separate me from the love of Christ.

I personally believe in a place called Purgatory. Where is that? The Bible isn't clear, scripture's not clear, even Catholic teaching isn't clear. I don't know the answer to that question. But I've had enough experiences with people in my life to know that there is some crossover and there is certainly some communication between those two realms. And if we believe, as the Apostles Creed says in the Communion of Saints, that when I say prayers and I ask for the intercession of saints, where are they? Are they real? Do I really believe that the saints are there to intercede for me in heaven? I do. So how is a ghostly appearance any different than the apparition of the saints, or a vision of a saint, or a vision of the Blessed Virgin coming to Medjugorje or wherever? There's so many unanswered questions. I just probably wouldn't say anything from the pulpit for fear of being labeled a Spiritist.

There is a scriptural warning and it must be in either first or second Samuel where Saul, in a whole lot of trouble, goes to the Witch of Endor and summons the prophet Samuel, and he comes back and it really ends up quite bad. God calls it sorcery and says divination is a sin and we shouldn't be doing this. In my experience, I didn't divine anything. I didn't hold a séance, I didn't grab a Ouija board—it just happened.

I'm not afraid of the spirit realm. St. Paul says we don't battle against flesh and blood, we battle against spirits, principalities, and powers of the air. They're out there. And some of them are not so benevolent, but greater is he who is in me than he who is in the world. I have no fear. I have heard stories of exorcisms and haunted places, where holy water chased the bad spirits out. I believe that there are things in the spirit world afoot that we can't see, but I fear them not. And because of the experience of my grandfather coming back and telling me that most interesting thing: "I'm in a wonderful place and everybody's here," I'm in no hurry to die, but I don't fear death. I have no fear of death. But like I said, I'm in no hurry for it to happen. [*Laughs.*] I hate to use a *Star Trek* word, but if one can't transport oneself from heavenly realms to the earthly realms, then how does Jesus get into that bread and wine every Sunday? These are things that are worthy for Christians to ponder and explore, and not be afraid of.

Have you had any supernatural experiences since?

I had a dream that was more crystal clear than the normal dream. I was asleep and shortly after my grandmother—Grandpa's wife— died, she came to me in a dream and I had not thought of the incident with my grandfather in years. I was in college when this happened, and I remember in the dream she looked young and beautiful, just like I remember my Grandpa looking. I said in the dream, "Hey, did you know that Grandpa came to visit me?" And she said, "Yes, he told me." And I thought that was kind of interesting. But that could've been just a dream—that was not an open-eyed, wide-awake experience.

I've heard a lot of stories from other people, but I haven't had any since. I guess the ghosts just don't like me anymore.

William Gilbert
Brooksville, Florida
September 5, 2004

In 2001, William Gilbert and his wife moved down to the small town of Brooksville, Florida, from Dayton, Ohio. The couple were expecting their first child, and William's wife wanted to be close to her mother when she had the baby. By September of 2004, William, his wife, and their 3-year-old son, Seth, had their fill of trying to reason with the hurricane season.

The autumn of 2004 was a particularly busy month for hurricanes in Florida, and during one evacuation, William and his wife saw a ghostly figure they will never forget. The 25-year-old shipping manager recalls the details leading up to the event.

What was the hurricane season like for you leading up to your encounter?

I can't remember how many storms had come through by that point because it's kind of a blur. I think [*Hurricane*] Charlie had come through and we evacuated for that, and I can't remember which one was next, but I think [*Hurricane*] Frances was the third.

It was getting kind of stressful with the constant evacuations and everything. The power had been out for days, and the heat was getting unbearable. When Frances was on its way, at first we were going to try to just ride it out—we lived in a mobile home, and we were going to ride it out.

As the storm started to get closer and closer, and the wind started to pick up, and the walls started creaking and popping, I started thinking, "Well if it were just me and my wife, that's one thing, but I can't take a risk with my son because he's not able to speak his own opinion about it." On September 2, we decided to go to some friend's of my mother- and father-in-law who lived in the next town, and we spent a good deal of time over there. I told them I felt like we were evacuating too early, but we spent the night with them.

If I remember correctly, the next afternoon they were saying on the radio that the storm seemed to be shifting a little bit, and my in-laws got it in their heads that we would just go back to their home so we could be more comfortable. We kind of felt like we were imposing on their friends, because me and my wife were with them and hadn't planned to be. So we all went back to my in-laws' home. At that point, we were going to try to fix dinner because things were starting to look a little bit better. But as the storm came in and got closer and closer to the coast, the wind started picking up and this particular area that we were in was just surrounded by hundreds of really, really tall—I'd say 80-foot (24 m)—pines, and I just didn't feel safe.

At one point I was standing on the back porch and the wind was whistling. It was coming in like waves, it kind of sounded like the ocean. And a tree snapped and collapsed onto the back porch, right down onto the middle of the house, and I was just terrified. I pretty much thought that was all she wrote for us.

This was when Frances actually came onto shore. I believe that was early afternoon of September 4th. So the tree fell right on the middle of my in-laws' home, and they lived in a modular home—it wasn't really much safer than our mobile home. So after the tree fell, all I could really think about was trying to get my son to a safe place. I happened to look over at their neighbor's house, and they lived in a brick home that was relatively new. I think it was only about 25 years old, and the way I saw it was that if a tree fell on their house, my son had a better chance of surviving than if it fell on this modular home that we were in.

I knew the neighbors. An older woman named Mrs. M. [*because of privacy issues, Gilbert asked that I simply refer to this woman as Mrs. M*]—I think she told me she was 89 or 90 years old—and her son and daughter lived there, and they were in their late 50s/early 60s. I had sat and talked to them often over the course of about three years. I remember when I first moved down to Florida I was having some car issues. As crazy as it sounds, Mrs. M. was an excellent driver, and I paid her to drive me back and forth to work for about two months until I was able to have the repairs done to my automobile. Occasionally she would send Christmas presents for my son, and coloring books, clothes that she would get from people that she knew. I knew her really well.

So I scooped my son up and I ran out the back door. I told my wife, "I'm taking Seth, and I'm going to try to make a run for the neighbor's house." I had to climb over a bunch of trees with him. That was a very scary ordeal because I remember a lot of power lines being down in the water, and I just kept thinking, "Please don't let a power surge happen while I'm standing in this puddle with my son."

So I got to the neighbors' house and they welcomed me in there, and shortly after that, my wife and her mother and father came over. The neighbors invited us to just go ahead and spend the night with them.

My in-laws, being that they're animal lovers to an almost ridiculous degree, had a houseful of dogs and cats and all kinds of things so they said, "We're going to kind of bounce between here and over there and we're going to try to spend the night over there to keep the animals calm. So the rest of us sat around and listened to the radio all night.

It got dark quick because the storm was blocking out the sun, and the trees are so tall it didn't get very bright back there anyways, even on a good day. I happened to ask where Mrs. M. was, because I thought it was peculiar that she wasn't home during this kind of weather. And they told me that she had died of natural causes the morning before.

What happened next is we sat around, and I didn't have a lot of batteries with me, but what I did have was starting to cut out. The flashlight started dying, the radio started dying, and everybody was getting tired so we decided to go ahead and call it a night—try and sleep through it, and when the storm passed out of the gulf side the next day, we could all go home and see if there was a house left.

When they were bringing out two small mattresses to put together to kind of make a bed for me, my wife, and son to sleep on, the daughter happened to mention that this was the bed that her mother had passed away in. That was a little bit creepy, I have to admit. I didn't want to know that. The next thing that happened was even a little creepier. They opened up the closet and pulled out a couple of pillows. And I know for a fact that those were the pillows that Mrs. M. had spent her final hours on. The pillows actually still had the indentation of the back of her head. [*Laughs.*] I just kind of fluffed them up and tried to concentrate on getting through the night. At this point I wasn't thinking anything strange or anything; I was just worried about the storm and wanted to get it over with. So we crawl on the mattress, and I'm laying on the right side and my wife is laying on the left side, and we have our son kind of sandwiched in between.

I remember falling asleep and being asleep for only an hour or two, because it was a really troubled type of sleep. Anybody that's been in a hurricane in Florida in September can vouch for the God-awful, sweltering heat. Once the power goes out for so many hours and the heat starts to filter through the house, it's hard to even breathe. I noticed that it seemed to be getting a little bit cooler, which registered pretty much right away that something didn't feel quite right. I'm not sure if what began to jar me from sleep was the slight temperature change or feeling my wife shake. When my wife gets scared, she'll shudder and shake, and it actually vibrates the bed. I could kind of feel the shake, and I opened my eyes and looked over to see what she was doing. She had a pretty tight grip on the blanket and was looking into the kitchen area.

I followed her gaze, and standing in front of the kitchen sink with her back to me was Mrs. M., who had been gone for just a little less than 48 hours at that point. She was standing there washing dishes was what she was doing. She was washing dishes. I don't know how else to say it other than to just come out and tell you what I saw. She didn't appear solid; she was slightly translucent. I could see the counter through her waist, and I could see the chrome of the sink. I could hear water running, and I could hear what sounded like spoons or forks kind of clinking off glass plates and this and that. I also heard humming, like she was entertaining herself with some kind of song.

How long did it last?

This lasted for maybe eight or nine seconds. I felt instantaneously nauseous and just terrified, really. I have to be honest—it doesn't sit well with me. I really felt trapped because there was no option, I had to stay there. I was thankful at the very least that I didn't feel threatened; she didn't do anything to seem hostile. She didn't move or make any steps or turn around to look at me or anything. She just stood there kind of humming to herself while she was washing dishes. She didn't acknowledge me at all, not in any way. I also noticed that even though the room was almost pitch-black, she was very well-defined. I could see her quite well, almost like she was producing her own luminescence. I don't know how to describe that, but it was about eight or nine seconds and then she just vanished—vanished right out of sight, and I looked over at my wife and she was terrified. I asked my wife if she saw that, and she acknowledged that she did and we didn't speak about it. We just laid there awake for the rest of the night with our son in between us. He never woke up; he was asleep during the whole thing.

Did you mention anything to the homeowners when you woke up?

No, I didn't. Mrs. M. died so recently that I felt they might think that I was saying it to try to make them feel better, like a "she's still with you" type of thing. I didn't want to come off as being insincere. So I never said anything to them about it, and me and my wife didn't speak about it for maybe a year.

In the morning, did you see anything in the sink?

There was a sink full of dirty dishes. I made a mental note of that when I was on my way out, I happened to glance over. I don't know what I expected to see. Maybe the dishes, maybe a clean sink, I don't know. But I did notice that it was full of some dishes, and I found it almost amusing because what an unusual thing to do. Of all of the things you could possibly do after you're dead, that somebody would catch you doing that, I found it kind of amusing. I guess it was just a lifetime of habit for her.

About a month after that, we decided we didn't want to deal with the storms anymore, so we packed it up and moved back here to Ohio.

Lee Prosser
Foyil, Oklahoma
Late December, 2001

Lee Prosser is 61 years old. He's a writer, artist, and musician who currently lives in Springfield, Missouri. Lee is also a sensitive—he claims he has seen, heard, or experienced spirits most of his life. But even for a sensitive, some encounters are more significant than others—such as the time Lee met with his father shortly after he passed away, but weeks before Lee received actual confirmation of his father's death.

When were you first aware that you could see spirits?

That'd probably be about age 6…between 5 and 6. But actually cognizant at 6. I would call it a change in peripheral vision. It seemed like I was able to see more than one would expect. I began to see shapes, and then outlines, and then persons.

Do you recall the first spirit you ever saw?

The first real one…I think that I can recall details. I must've been 6, and I was at my grandmother Firestone's mansion in Springfield, Missouri. She had one of these really old Victorian, real Gothic-type houses. Three-story. I was going down into the basement, and there was a man there. He was old and had one of those handlebar mustaches. He said hello to me and I said hello back and I went on my way.

I told my Uncle Willard about it, and he explained it to me in terms that I could understand. He said not to be afraid of such things, that it was just part of another existence—another doorway. He didn't mean a doorway in the sense that there was a doorway that opened, but using it as an analogy to say they came through, or they passed through. That's when I began to understand that seeing spirits was normal.

Uncle Willard made it possible for me to realize that such things were not evil; they were as valid as you and I talking on the phone, except in another otherworldly dimension. He taught me not to label. You go through life, you get pro-grammed, you get socialized, but you still label. But he taught me not to label that which I did not understand, until I could understand it.

Let's talk about your parents, specifically your father. When did your dad leave?

I think I was 2 years old when they separated, and I think they divorced when I was 7. At least by 7 years of age, he was out of my life.

What do you remember of him?

Nothing. Not until I was in my mid-20s and he visited me once in Santa Monica, California.

What was your dad like?

Let me give you a perspective at age 61, how's that? [*Laughs.*] I think he was a very charismatic Irishman. He loved to drink, he loved women, and he did both very well because he was what you would call a Tyrone Power-type of physical specimen. He was a good-looking man. My dad was a Navy Seabee in World War II, and he earned the Bronze Star at one point.

I did have contact with him when I was in my 30s. He lived back here for…oh, a couple of years. By then he had been through several wives. I can't even remember what the last one's name was. But oddly enough, when he died, he died with the first wife that he divorced my mother for. [*Laughs.*] He had married her twice over a period of 30 years or so.

I did see my dad at one other point later in life. He made a trip back here to Missouri, and when I saw him, it did not occur to me at the time that it was him because he had a full, dark beard. But there was something about his voice. I saw him in a bookstore. He came in and he sold some books. A friend owned a bookstore and I just stepped in to help, and I was positive it was my dad. He gave no acknowledgment that it was him, but to this day I know it was him. He sold some books on gardening—he was quite a gardener.

I just felt a gut feeling because I hadn't seen him for years and years, and now he had this thick, bushy beard. He looked like he was more stooped and he never acknowledged me or anything, but I come to find out from other people that he had been here in Missouri during that month. It seems he'd come back to visit or see different people.

When did you experience your father's spirit?

Actually, he came to me. The visit happened just after Christmas of 2001. Deborah [*Lee's wife*] and I were living in Foyil, Oklahoma. I was sitting in my living room and I saw my dad standing there.

Do you remember what he looked like?

Yeah, I do…I do and I don't. I thought he had a Navy peacoat on, and he had one of those little acrylic knit caps that you pull over your head to go outdoors with, and boots—they were shiny. Jeans. It seemed like he had this confounded dark beard on, too. When he first appeared he didn't have the beard, and then later on he did. I'm still puzzled over that.

We had a dialogue, and I knew he was dead. He was still trying to make peace with me. He was trying to apologize for never having been there. I was sitting there and he just appeared. I could connect his voice. He had a very charismatic voice…it was kind of a light, husky voice. It was him. He was the last person I expected to see again, even dead, really. I had forgiven him a long time ago. I mean, you know you can't carry a grudge against somebody that walked out of your life and was never there. Well, I guess you can, but it's a lot of work.

I'd never really given him walking out much thought, and I told him so. I said, "Hey, that's the past, you've got nothing to worry about. Go on." I'm sure I said more than that, because it lasted awhile.

I think there has got to be some kind of link—a time link involved in which the person that's coming to visit either is not allowed voluntarily, or involuntarily, to stay more than a certain length of time. I have come to believe that over these many years because I can remember being visited by my Uncle Les, who was a favorite uncle of mine, and it seems like what we perceive as time, to them, may be more limited. It's kind of like they're making stops. The train stops here to see Lee, the train stops here to see so-and-so, and it seems like they have a transition period.

When I saw my dad, it wasn't one of these long, dragged-out things that last for an hour or two hours. It passed very quickly. I know he was very…I don't want to use the words "contrite" or "penitent"…but it was kind of a state of being at ease and saying some things that he'd wanted to say all of his life since he was divorced from my mother. As I recall, and I hadn't seen them, but I think dad had other children and other wives, but I was his first born. I guess given the old school of thought before World War II, the first born was most important.

When was it confirmed for you that he had really died?

He died December 22, 2001. I have it written in my Bible. But I think it was a full month before I heard. That's when my mother contacted me because she had found out. She said she had been contacted by his spirit, too, so I guess he was making amends to the whole damn world. [*Laughs.*]

Did you think your dad was dead when you saw him back in December of 2001?

Yes, there was no doubt because he just came. People just don't appear in the middle of your house. [*Laughs.*] I knew he was dead, and I sensed what he was there for. I reassured him that I had forgiven him a long time ago. I mean, there is nothing to be ashamed of. He had a life, and that's the way his life was. He was just a wild and woolly Irishman.

Robert Allen
Huron, South Dakota
December 1971

Robert Allen has been in entertainment his entire adult life. He's been a hypnotist and magician, but he got his start as a musician, playing guitar in a Chicago-based band that toured throughout the United States. The 58-year-old claims to have had many encounters throughout his life, but he's never forgotten a visitation he had when he was staying in a hotel in Huron, South Dakota.

What were you doing in Huron?

I had to be around 22 years old or somewhere around there, and I was in Huron. We were playing at a supper club—I had a band with my wife. My grandmother at that time was probably in her late 80s…well, she was 89 when she died, so she had to be 89. I called home once in a while, but at that age you know how you are—you're not thinking too much about Grandpa and Grandma, so it wasn't something that was in my thoughts.

That night I went to sleep and we were laying there sleeping, and in my dream I saw my Grandma reaching out for me. She never spoke English. She never really learned to speak other than a couple of little words here and there. My grandfather kept her at home and she was the typical Italian wife who stayed home cooking and doing dishes. She always called me "Bop-ee," because she couldn't pronounce "Bobby." In my dream I saw her reaching out to me and going, "Bop-ee, Bop-ee." It frightened me and I woke up. I sat straight up in the bed and my wife at the time said, "What's the matter?" I said, "My grandmother just came to me in a dream." And she said, "Oh, you're having a nightmare." I said, "No, it was really weird, she was reaching out to me like she wanted me to come to her."

Just as we finished that discussion, the phone rang. My mom always knew where we were at, and she called. She said, "It's Mom." And I said, "Yeah?" She said, "We're at the hospital with Grandma. She just passed away." I said, "Oh my god, she just came to me in a dream." She said, "Really?" And she told me that the last thing my Grandma did before she died was she looked around the room because I wasn't there. She said, "Where's Bop-ee?"

Right there I knew she'd come to say goodbye.

How did you feel when you realized that this was more than a dream?

It scared me at first, but after I got comfortable with it, I realized it was wonderful. It's been something that's been a place to go when I want to get peaceful. My grandmother pretty much raised me as a kid. My mom and dad were working two jobs each, so I spent probably 75 percent of my time with my grandparents until I was 10 or 12 years old.

It was an amazing incident, and I've never forgotten about it. I've had so many of these different encounters that at first I used to get spooked by them, but now I'm actually very comforted by it. It doesn't scare me anymore.

Kathy Flaherty
Hog Island, Rhode Island
Late June 2002

Kathy Flaherty is a 33-year-old wife and mother of two children who lives in Millis, Massachusetts. She lost her mother to cancer on June 9, 2002, and the loss took a heavy toll on her and her family. Kathy believes she has received several subtle signs from her mother since she passed. But one sign left her family shaken.

Tell me about your mom.

She was this Italian woman, and family was her entire life. She was the whole core of this family and when she left, the whole dynamic of the family changed. It's just very empty now. My mother was at New England Baptist Hospital, and from her room she could see all of the airplanes taking off [*from Logan airport in Boston*], and she would sit in the bed and say, "Oh, I'm just wondering where all of these people are going." She'd make up her own story for them, wonder what destination they were going to. That's kind of how she passed her time, looking out the window.

When the hospital called us and told us she was dying, my brother, my sister, and I were on our way into Boston. We were driving up the VFW Parkway, and then we had taken a right onto the main road heading up to the hospital. The hospital is on a hill and there was this cloud and, honest to God, it was right over the hospital and there were sunbeams over the hospital, and then the clouds just closed. When it closed, I remember thinking...*she's gone*. And that was almost the exact time that she died.

What kinds of other signs were you getting?

They may sound insignificant now, but when we were in the funeral home and we were saying our last goodbyes to her before they closed the casket, my sister approached the casket and a song from the Mamas & the Papas came on in the lobby of the funeral parlor—"Leaving on a Jet Plane." Even to this day it just tears me apart, the coincidence.

My mother passed away June 9, 2002, and after the funeral and all that, my whole family went down to our summerhouse. It's a small community down there, so all our friends and family popped in on Friday night. It was probably a bigger group than normal because they were showing support. The house is still kind of under construction—so it's not really airtight or soundproof or anything. My dad is building the whole thing, so if a dime drops upstairs, you can hear it. I had tucked the kids into bed upstairs. I tucked Lydia, who was 2 1/2 years at the time—I put her in the Pack 'n Play. And then my daughter, Bridgett, who was 3 1/2 months, I put her on my parents' double bed, which probably wasn't the best thing, but she didn't roll at that age. I kind of rolled little blankets around the side of her—to box her in—and then put her to sleep. She was sound asleep on the bed and we all went downstairs to be with the group.

My husband was about to leave to go next door to play a game of cards or something and I said to him, "If you don't mind, just pop upstairs and check the kids before you go next-door," because we figured we'd check on them every 15 or 20 minutes. He said, "Yeah, no problem."

We were probably downstairs for only 20 minutes to a half an hour max before he went upstairs to check the kids. I'm sitting there talking to my friends, and all of a sudden we hear the baby crying. And then she [*started*] screaming, and so I went up there. I said, "Did you wake the baby up?"

My husband was holding the baby and he looked at me and he was completely pale white. He had this awful face on, he was so shaken up. He said, "Kathy, I know you've been saying you've been seeing signs about your mother this past week." And he said, "Kathy, the baby was sound asleep across the room. I first thought somebody stole her, and then I looked and she was sound asleep over here."

She was only 3 1/2 months old—she doesn't crawl, she doesn't roll. We didn't hear a thump...we didn't hear anything.

What did your husband think happened?

He wasn't a big believer in all of the signs I thought I was getting right after my mom died, but this was so freaky to him. He said, "I can't believe it." I said, "Was she awake?" He said, "Kathy, she was sound asleep and she looked beautiful." I know that sounds odd.

Where did he find the baby?

The baby was kind of right under the insulation. The insulation is on the wall, and she was at the foot of that, where the wall meets the floor. We're talking about six feet (2 m) from the bed. And our other daughter, who was only 2 1/2, was sound asleep in the Pack 'n Play.

My friend Kim, who is a nurse, came up from downstairs. Kim checked the baby head-to-toe because when babies fall—especially onto a hardwood floor, which is what was in the room—you can see whether they hit their head, or their arm, or whatever. She looked at her and said she didn't even have a red mark to show that she fell. Kim looked up and her eyes got all filled up and she said, "It's like your mother carried her to the floor safely and was holding her up here." We were all so emotional because we can't explain what happened. She was only a newborn and she was just moved.

I can't explain to you in words, but it was like the most peaceful feeling in the bedroom that night. Here's my friend Kim, myself, and my husband, and his eyes just filled up. I can't explain the peacefulness the room felt. The way that the lighting was, the whole feeling of it was like my mother was there.

That house was my mom's place. That was where she and my dad spent their entire summers.

Jim Demick
Rockwood, Michigan
September 2005

Jim Demick is a 32-year-old who recently graduated art school and now manages a car detailing facility. His passion is illustrating comics and cartoons, but he also draws portraits, and pursues other artistic endeavors.

When a spirit encounter happens, we rarely have a camera poised ready to capture what we saw, so the moment is often lost…unless you're an artist who can recreate that moment. This was the case after Jim woke up face-to-face with a ghost.

When did this happen?

It was September of 2005. I was fast asleep, and in the middle of the night I just opened my eyes and there was a face, I mean maybe an inch away from my face. I was lying on my side and just opened my eyes and there it was. It just scared the hell out of me, pretty much. It was just shock.

It wasn't until a few days later that I started piecing it together, because a friend of mine had a very similar experience and she found out that it was a family member of hers that came to visit her. And I started thinking, well, you know, the shape of the face, the features, and the way the hair was done looks similar to my aunt or my mother—they had the same haircut and everything.

There wasn't a lot of detail. It was just kind of a pale, translucent-like…you can see through it, and it kind of reminded me of the mask from the *Scream* movies. You couldn't see the eyes or the mouth, but you could make out the outline, the shape of the face, the cheeks, and the hair. It was short hair, but it didn't have any color to it. It was more of a whitish kind of translucent. I didn't really see the whole head; it was maybe from the upper lip up, like she was crouched down on the side of the bed looking up at me.

"When I rolled over in my bed I saw what appeared to be the pale, translu-cent-like form of my aunt peeking at me." Illustration by Jim Demick.

Did you tell anyone about the experience the next day?

Yeah, I told a few friends what happened. I was pretty-well woken up after that [*laughs*]. It was roughly two or three in the morning.

A few people were asking me what it looked like, and I thought it resembled my aunt. I was told a good 10 to 15 years ago by a supposed psychic that my aunt was watching over me. And she passed away. I believe I was a senior in high school when she died—that was 1992.

How did she die?

It was a heart attack. She was getting ready for work, coming to take my mom—they worked together—and she was putting her socks on. She sat down on the bed and just died right there.

Were you close to her?

We were pretty close. She was my favorite aunt growing up. We lived right down the street from her and my mom worked with her every day, so I saw her all the time.

When did the psychic tell you that your aunt was watching over you?

I think that was around '94. It was actually an ex-girlfriend that was into witchcraft and this and that. She really knew a lot about the paranormal, and that's kind of what got me into it more. I'm still kind of a skeptic about it, but that's what she told me and that kind of stuck with me ever since she said that. And then I happen to see that—see her image that night—and when I woke up, it seemed to make sense.

Did your psychic girlfriend know about your aunt?

Not really. She never met her or anything. We did a whole psychic thing—the tarot card reading, all that. She actually told me that my aunt was watching over me. I hadn't mentioned anything about my aunt. My aunt had been dead for a good two, maybe three years, and I never brought it up. We didn't really talk about it, my girlfriend brought it up, which kind of shocked me.

What do you make of the whole experience now?

I would lean it toward a quick visit. Or maybe she's always there and I just happened to see her when I wasn't supposed to. I've heard when you're in that half-awake, half-asleep stage you can see things that you normally wouldn't see. That's what I kind of chalked it up as. She didn't really give me signs or anything; she was just there and gone. I just chalk it up as that. I haven't seen her since then.

Did you tell your mom about the experience?

No…no. My parents aren't really believers in the paranormal whatsoever. They're old-fashioned; they don't want to get into that.

This whole thing left me unsettled the first night, maybe two nights. I was kind of, "What the heck was that?" But the more I thought about it, the more calm I got about it, and the more I accepted. I can't say for definite it was my aunt, but I'm almost positive it was. That's who it resembled.

Heather Coker
New Palestine, Indiana
2005

The years 2004 and 2005 were difficult ones for 32-year-old Heather Coker, a writer living outside of Indianapolis. Her uncle Mark passed away, and she was having trouble with her marriage, which led her to some destructive behavior. On several occasions since her uncle's passing, Heather has sensed his presence, and even heard him. She feels he was able to help her through a rough period in her life.

Were you close to your uncle Mark?

Yeah, actually he was pretty close with all of his nieces—he didn't have children of his own. All of his life he was always the kind of guy who would give the shirt off his back. He always had big things about family always sticking together, that kind of thing—it was always foremost on his mind; being around the family, especially during the holidays and special occasions. He'd come over to make as many visits as he possibly could.

He passed away in February of 2004. He was only 44. He was pretty young—it came as quite a shock to all of us girls. My cousin had found him—he had died in my grandma's house and my cousin started having a severe panic attack. It's kind of a joke right now that we can sort of laugh about. The ambulance took her out of the house and to the hospital before they got him out.

It was pretty strange because at the funeral all of us girls were talking. My cousin found him at about three o'clock, and we were talking about how we each had a severe migraine hit us around that time. I had mentioned how I had gotten this really big headache and I felt like something was really, really wrong. And this was before anybody had called us. My dad called me around nine o'clock that night to let me know what had happened.

A lot of us, especially the girls, have been having encounters with him ever since he had passed on…like when we needed him, and if we were in a depression, or going through bad times, or something like that, it would always feel like he was right there with us.

What hard times were you experiencing after his death?

I had been going through a very bad time with my marriage, and it was pretty much the second time. I had just about had enough of it and I was about ready to end the marriage. But it was other things that I was doing to myself. I wasn't really thinking about the way I was dealing with a lot of the problems.

I was sitting at my kitchen table like I usually did, working on some writing, and just kind of thinking about a lot of things that were going on. It was kind of a shock for me. At first I thought I was hearing my brother's television going off because I thought I heard some noises. So I was like, "Okay, what's going on?" I thought maybe he'd gotten up to get ready for work, so I was kind of trying to put that out of my head so I could focus on some writing, and all of a sudden I just heard this voice. It was as if somebody was in the living room, which is right next to the kitchen, screaming at me, "If you keep that…stuff…up, before the day's over you're going to be dead." [*Laughs.*] But he didn't say "stuff."

I froze for a second. I was just like, "Oh my God," because it sounded exactly like my uncle. I jumped up from my seat and ran into the living room because I thought maybe somebody was playing a joke on me or something like that. I didn't see anybody in the living room and I was like, "Okaaay…." I was trying to figure out where I could have heard it.

What kind of stuff do you think the voice was referring to?

At the time I was trying to get off of ephedrine, and at that point I was basically cutting myself down from overdosing. But sooner or later I knew it was going to catch up with me anyway.

After I heard the voice, I remember trying to figure out what this was. After things had calmed down a little bit, and I was able to compose myself, I went to go knock on my brother's door and ask him to take me to the hospital.

A few months later, I had gone to therapy to talk about that incident, because it had been giving me a lot of panic attacks. I was telling the therapist about what I had heard and he was pretty amazed. He was telling me that usually if people hear voices, they aren't as constructive as that, you know, to try and help people out. Most of the time they're usually pretty much detrimental. He asked me what did I think it was. I said if it wasn't my survival instinct kicking in and scaring the heck out of me, it had to have been my uncle because that voice. It just had this very deep quality that only he had. You know, one of those low, growling-type voices. I had never heard him get angry in my life, but [*that's*] just the way it affected me when I heard that.

Ever since then, after I had finally come to my senses and decided to end the marriage, I went to move over to my grandma's house. I'd still feel that same kind of feeling I had when I heard that voice, but when I came over here, it was more of a peaceful feeling, like, "You're safe, you're home now, you're a lot better." I can still kind of hear that voice in the back of my mind, but it's not so bad. And most of the time when I hear that, I start to feel like he's around. Really close.

So you feel it's less of a warning and more of a comforting presence now?

Yeah, it's definitely been comforting. And I've had a couple of experiences since then. I've actually felt like he's come up and placed his hand on my shoulder if I'd be sitting at the computer looking around. I'd really feel like there'd be somebody here with me that's kind of comforting me.

What makes you think it's your uncle?

A lot of it is the feeling I get. And a lot of the time…. [*Laughs.*] Especially if I'm alone in my room or something after I clean up, I'd hear pennies dropping from the ceiling or somewhere.

One time, it was in October, just before I had to go to a court session, and I was so nervous about that, because I didn't really know what was going on with it. I knew it would have to be about money or something, so I had just cleaned up my room and I decided I was going to try and take a nap and de-stress, and I heard two pennies dropping from the ceiling. I looked over and I saw them both in the middle of the floor, heads up. There wasn't anywhere that the pennies could've dropped from, and it wasn't my cats because they were lying right next to me, I'm thinking, "Okay, it's my uncle either telling me it's going to be all right, or he's playing around to try and get my mind off things."

We've had a lot of instances where the family would come around and they have a penny show up somewhere, so we know it was him because he always had this thing about picking up every penny that he found. When he was alive he'd say, "Oh, there's a penny!" He didn't care if it was heads up or tails up. He'd say, "Oh, it's a penny...they add up pretty quick." And I'd say, "Yeah, they sure do." [*Laughs.*]

What did you think when you saw the pennies?

It was funny because after I saw those pennies I said, "That's awful nice, but it would sure be better if you could drop me a quarter or something like that. That'd be a little more helpful." [*Laughs.*]

I was getting up to go write about it, and not long after that I heard another coin dropping and I haven't been able to find that one since. So I said, "Okay, if that one's a quarter, he's making me look for that one." That would definitely be like his sense of humor. It was just like I got this really good sense of peace that it was family around me.

Since going to therapy, and being able to talk about it a little more, and putting it a little bit more behind me, I have that feeling that my family is still around with me.

Sierra Gregoire
Benson, Vermont
June 1999

Sierra Gregoire, now 11 years old, was only 5 years old when she lost her Uncle Jimmy. Shortly after he died, both Sierra and her father saw Uncle Jimmy, who came for one last visit.

Sierra's mother, 38-year-old Debbie Robbins, spoke first about her brother, Jimmy.

He was 28 years old, and he committed suicide. We're not really sure why; he didn't leave a note or anything. He was into snowmobiling, he was a semi-pro racer. He was also into motorcycles. He was young and he was quite popular—he had a ton of friends. There were over 300 people at his funeral. He had a lot going for him, or so we thought. June 9, 1999, was when he died.

He had come up [*that previous*] Memorial Day weekend. My dad lives up near me, so Jimmy had come up to visit my father. We had owned a camp in the next town up together, and they were all up there, and I didn't make it up to visit because I was really sick that day. Jimmy had gone home the next day before I got to see him. It was seven days later that he shot himself.

He was living with my mom in Manchester, Vermont, and I had gone down to be with her when I found out. Sierra was just in kindergarten when it happened. It was actually the last day of school.

At this point, I asked Sierra what she remembers of the day she found out her Uncle Jimmy had died.

I stayed at home with my dad, and my mom went to go visit my grandmother. When I was that little, I hated sleeping alone, so I slept with Dad. It was a normal night and nothing really big happened, and we just went to bed. It was around 10:30, and I woke up out of a dead sleep. I sat straight up and Uncle Jimmy was just sitting at the end of my bed, and I got really, really scared. I just went under the covers. I woke up my dad, and he told me to get out from under the covers and go back to sleep, and I said that I can't—I'm too scared; I see Uncle Jimmy at the end of my bed.

What did he look like?

He looked exactly like I had known him, but I really didn't get to see him that much. He was wearing a plaid shirt—really all I saw was his top half. He looked bluish and silvery.

I was so scared, I just wanted to fall asleep. I didn't want to know what was going on. So I put my hands over my ears, and I closed my eyes real tight, and I tried to go to sleep. I ended up falling asleep, but I did have dreams about him, like Jimmy being there with me as a ghost and everything, and that scared me, too.

When I woke up in the morning I was still a little shaky, but I went down to the kitchen table and sat down. My dad told me that breakfast would be ready soon, and then he sat down and he handed me a plate and I started eating. I couldn't take the silence, and I asked him if he believed me when I told him that Uncle Jimmy was at the end of my bed, and he said, "Yeah." My dad said that Uncle Jimmy said that he loved me and he missed me.

Sierra says she's never experienced anything ghostly either before or after that incident with her uncle. I asked Robbins if she remembers her daughter and husband telling her about seeing Jimmy.

Honestly, when they first told me, I thought that he came to say goodbye to me, and I wasn't there. Because I was at my mom's. I mean, I don't know. I have no idea. But that was my first thought. Of course, I was devastated at the time.

When I got home, I do remember her dad telling me about it, but he didn't describe her as being scared. I know she said she was scared, but he said she just woke up and said that Uncle Jimmy was standing at the bottom of the bed. And he said he saw him, too. I don't remember her dad saying that Jimmy spoke to him.

Sierra, however, remembered the day differently, and offered the following:

I do.

Suzy Lehman
Jasper, Tennessee
1997 to 1998

Suzy Lehman is a 42-year-old accountant who has lived in the town of Jasper, Tennessee, most of her life. She's an animal lover who has always had pets around her, though one particular cat was more special than some of the others. Suzy, her husband, Keith, and her son, Jordan, have all seen this special cat (and one of her kittens), even after the cats passed away. The ghosts we know aren't always human—sometimes our pets come back, too.

How did this cat come into your life?

I came home from work one day, and she was sitting on the front porch waiting on me. It was probably 1985, and she never left. I mean she was there with me forever. She was with me through my divorce. She was a blue-gray cat that had big green eyes, and her name was Kitty. After she was with me for a while, her name became Fat Kitty because she became fat. She was a very, very fat cat.

Kitty, before she found me, she had been abused. Both of her front paws had been broken, and neither one of them had been set. One of them didn't straighten out, and the other one set at an odd angle.

She was a very unique cat, and I've never felt as connected to an animal as I did to her. I've always had animals. We don't have any pets right now, but this is the first time in my whole life. She was the one that I had always felt the most connection to, her and the two kittens of hers that we kept. Fat Kitty was with me for probably about 15 years. The vet figured she was probably a year old, maybe a year and a half old when I found her...or when she found me. I didn't find her, she found me.

After she died, and she died very suddenly, it was real traumatic for me. We were living about four blocks from where we are now when she died. I was just frantic. It was like a mother losing a child.

When did you start experiencing Fat Kitty's ghost?

You would see her. You would be in the bathroom, or you would think you'd catch a glimpse of her out of the corner of your eye. Nothing really particular—just vague things. And you'd think, "Well, it was just my imagination." Until this one night when I literally...I felt her jump on my bed. Then two or three days later, my husband said he had felt her jump, too. He just mentioned to me; it was like, "You know, I thought she jumped on the bed." We both thought it was just one of those weird things. It was when I was pregnant with my son that she came and spent the night with us—when we felt her jump on the bed.

Initially we started questioning ourselves, because when I first started seeing Fat Kitty, I saw her a whole lot right after she died because I was upset. And then she went away for a little while; we wouldn't see her as much. And then I started seeing her more when I was pregnant. And the longer I was pregnant, the more complications I developed, and we all just assumed I was seeing her because I was stressed out. I figured Keith was seeing her because he was stressed out about me. And for a long time, neither one of us said anything. When we finally admitted to each other that we were seeing the cat. [*Laughs.*] It had been going on for a while. And then we were like, "Okay, we've been seeing her again."

Then, our son was born. He was a preemie, so there was a lot of concern about whether or not he was going to be okay. After he was born, you would go in the bedroom—we had his bassinet in our bedroom—and you would think for a second that you saw Fat Kitty laying up underneath the bassinet.

After a little while, we started noticing that, when you would go in the room after you made the bed, the foot of our bed closest to the bassinet would be messed up, like the cat had been lying there. I always thought it was just one of those things. You think, "Well, I'm just imagining it."

When our son was about 10 months old, we moved back to the house where I grew up. My son actually sleeps in the bedroom that I slept in before I got married. When we moved, we inherited three cats from my mom and dad; we inherited two of Fat Kitty's kittens—they were full-grown cats at that point—and a third cat that mom and dad had.

Jordan always talked about playing with the kitties, and we'd ask him, "Which one do you like best?" And he said he liked the one that couldn't walk. Now, the other three could walk fine. One night Jordan started describing to my husband and I how that last cat ran. He mimicked her. She had that one leg that didn't straighten, and I'm like, "Okay, so it's not all our imagination. Jordan's really been seeing her."

Jordan's a very unique child—he just turned eight. He saw Fat Kitty all the time. Keith and I would see her out of the corner of our eye, like running up the steps, or running down the steps, or walking by a doorway—you'd turn and see movement out of the corner of your eye. Jordan literally would see her. And Jordan could describe how fat she was.

Until we put up the Christmas tree this year, we hadn't seen her ghost in probably two or three years, but this year, this was the strangest thing. When I had Fat Kitty, she had one litter of kittens, and I kept two of the kittens out of the litter. One of them was a calico that we named Calico. Calico was fascinated by Christmas trees.

One afternoon, and this was just a few weeks ago, I was in the house completely by myself and was walking through our living room. I stopped and was looking at the tree, you know, making sure I had everything the way I wanted it decorated, and all of a sudden, one of the ornaments on the bottom of the tree started moving. That's what Calico always loved to do; she loved to run by and slap an ornament, or lay up underneath it and slap it.

I don't know what made me do this, but I looked at that ornament and I said, "Calico, just leave the tree alone!" And it stopped immediately. My husband saw it do the same thing. It was always one particular ornament on one particular part of the tree that she used to play with. We got to the point where we would say, "Just leave the tree alone, Calico. Just leave it." When I first saw the ornament move, I said, "Oh God, it's gonna start again."

What do you make of living with the ghost of a cat, or cats?

I've never been one to believe in ghosts. I'm not comfortable with hauntings, all that kind of thing. For so many years before Jordan was able to talk about it, I always figured it was just my attachment to Fat Kitty that made me think I was seeing her. Then everybody was seeing her—even my mom and dad had caught glimpses of her a time or two when they were at our house when Jordan was small. I don't know what to make of it. It's just weird.

I was brought up in the South, in a religious, church-going background, and you don't talk about ghosts, you don't talk about spirits, you don't talk about psychic ability, or any other thing like that. You don't talk about the paranormal. It doesn't exist. And then when it comes into your home, you go, "Okay, it really does exist."

Michael Wright
Salem, Virginia
November 17, 2005

Michael Wright was close to his sister her entire life. For most of his adult life, the 53-year-old worked in a traveling circus. "Not a carnival, now—a circus with elephants and lions and tigers," he said. "I was a stilt walker. I was, like, 15 (4.6 m) feet up in the air. I did clowning; I was a producing clown on the show. I had a motorized bathtub, and I spun plates."

Being on the road, he wasn't always as close to family as he liked to be, but after retiring from the circus in the mid-1990s, he had more time to be with his family. He and his partner, Ray, retired to Milton, Florida.

Wright is also a shutterbug. His digital camera goes with him just about everywhere, and he has actively pursued spirit photography—the concept of using a camera to capture the image of (or partial image or residue from) a ghost or spirit. After his sister, Trisha, passed away on November 12, 2005, he never intended to capture her spirit image, but he was shocked with one photo he took.

What was Trisha like?

She was born and raised in Salem, Virginia. She worked for the L'eggs company, you know the ladies nylons—she was a district manager for them.

When we were kids, we had horses. My mother and father had Appaloosa horses, and my mom did barrel racing. You know what barrel racing is? You're on the horse, they give you a signal, and you race the horse down, go around the barrel as sharp as you can, and turn back and go around another barrel sharp as you can, and then you make a long run to the gate where you start from. They use a time clock to see how fast you can go. Men and women did it, but my mom had a specialty in that.

When I was growing up, I couldn't care less about horses. Though when we had friends and neighbors over, then I wanted to get on the pony and show off like anybody else. We lived up in the country for about 12 years or 14 years of my life. I liked it there.

When my sister got older, about 12 years ago she had gastric-bypass surgery. Before she went in, she told me, "Mike, if anything ever happens, please spread my ashes up there where I had the most joy in my life." I said "Where is that?" And she goes, "Up in the country." And I said, "Okay, fine."

Well, she had the gastric bypass, they lost her, and they brought her back. I was so afraid she was going to die. And it didn't look too good, but she made it through that. I told my dad, when it didn't look good, I said, "Well, Dad, I want to make sure she gets her wishes." He said, "Well, Mike, she's not even dead yet." I said, "I know, but I just want to make sure," you know?

So everything came out of the surgery okay. But after that, Trish found out she had breast cancer. Because she lost all this weight, then she found a lump in her breast. So she got that taken care of, and five years later, she gets another lump in her other breast. By the time they found it, she had spots on her lungs, and then from there it went into her liver. After that, she was taking chemo and radiation for over a year or so. She's cried to me over the phone before, saying, "I'm in such bad pain, I just want to die. I can't take the pain." I said, "Trish, it'll be fine." But I didn't know what she was going through. I never experienced it.

She was born March 12, 1950, and she passed November 12, 2005, on a Saturday. Before she passed, I came up from Florida and got to spend a day and a half with her—overnight and all. I helped to feed her. She was so coherent just the night before. But the next morning when I got there at 10:30, her eyes were wide open and she had this heavy breathing. I knew she was going into the death rattle. Her son, Jason, was there. So I put a chair on each side of the bed. I put the flowers in front of her so she could see the flowers, and I sat down and I started talking to her. I started rubbing her hand and all. When she sleeps, she always put her thumb inside of her fist and balls her fist up. So I stuck my two fingers down inside of her fist and I said, "You know, it's okay to go, Trish. Dad's okay. Jason's a big boy, and I can watch after Dad if I have to." I said, "You just go ahead and go. Momma's right there in front of you. Can you see her?" And she'd nod her head yes. I said, "Well you just go ahead and let go, because it's fine. You don't have to suffer anymore." And within three minutes she was gone.

After she passed, we were at the funeral home and I said, "I don't know what her wishes were, but I know what her wish was when she got the gastric bypass. She wanted to be cremated." Jason had said he also knew that she wanted to be cremated. They had a couple debates about what to do with the ashes. She told me that she wanted to make sure that I spread the ashes up in the country where we had the horses. So I said I thought the ashes should be spread on the property.

Since the incident they had in southern Georgia with the crematorium [*referring to the Noble, Georgia, crematory incident of 2002 where more than 100 corpses were discovered on the property—the owners claimed the bodies were never incinerated because the equipment wasn't work-*

ing correctly], they now put a brass tag in with the ashes clarifying who she was…I've got it right here. After they cremated her, what they did was they buried an empty urn—which the family members don't know. It's only my father and I, Jason, and my partner, Ray, knows that.

I asked Jason, "When do you want to go up there? And he said, "Let's make sure it's a nice day." So we went up there on the 17th.

At one time, the property in Salem was connected on the borderline with my grandparents' property. And now my cousin owns that property. Now the fence is down—it used to be a barbed-wire fence, but all that's gone. It's been 20-something years now. So I walked over to the property where I thought that the riding ring was where we used to ride the horses in. And I said this is a good spot right here. So I opened the urn—it was a plastic urn and there was a plastic bag—so I open the plastic bag and I said, "Well, here you are, Trish. This is where you wanted to be, and this is where you're going to be." I sprinkled the ashes. And of course I was in tears, and I was just talking to her and telling her how much I loved her and all.

When we were done, I picked up the plastic urn and the bag and I was walking away and I said, "You know, I should take a picture of where I spread the ashes so I can remember." So I took a couple of pictures, I looked down at the little LED screen, and I couldn't believe what I saw. I said, "Oh my gosh, what's this?"

I was facing the north/northeast and the sun was behind me, and that's when I took the photograph. I know for a fact that can't be sun glare. There's no possible way. Not what I'm getting here.

Did you see that misty form with your naked eye or only after you took the picture?

115

The photo Michael took of the spot where he spread his sister's ashes.
Photo by Michael Wright.

No. I took the picture first. I couldn't see anything. I was just taking the picture of the area where I spread the ashes, and I clicked a couple of times, and I looked down at the LCD screen to make sure that I got the picture.

What do you think is in this picture?

I think that she was going up to heaven. Between you and me. She's going into the other plane. To me, I think your soul goes up to heaven—your soul goes up, but your imprint of what you've done in your life and all of that, goes into another plane. That's what I believe in.

Chapter 3

Ghosts on the Job

Photo source: "Dark Hallway" © istockphoto.com/Roosevelt Francois

Working folks have to put up with the demands of their jobs—the rude customers, the overbearing bosses, and sometimes even the ghosts. Ghosts are rarely in job descriptions, and though their presence can add a lot of character (and even a customer draw) to a business, they can be stressful and frightening for employees who didn't expect to encounter them.

There are no rules as to when, how, or why a ghost sighting may occur. Some spirits may be intrigued at the human activity happening in the places they once called home or work, but others may be attached to the land, or may be drawn to a specific person.

Jeff Revis
Dayton, Tennessee
1985

When Jeff Revis was 25 years old, he was hired by the city of Dayton, Tennessee, as a laborer. He never did like factory work, and the mowing and dusty outdoors labor was wreaking havoc on his allergies. Jeff put in for something indoors, and when an opportunity came up to work the graveyard shift at the water plant, he took it. For the first few weeks, he worked the day shift while they trained him, then he switched over to nights.

Revis was a believer in ghosts years before he started working at the water plant. When he was about 10 years old, he rode his bicycle around the side of the church located next-door to his family's home and encountered a man wearing robes who simply looked out of place. He threw his bicycle down and ran home. He jokes now that he wishes he could have more ghost experiences, because he's fascinated by the topic. He admits, however, that he hopes to never encounter again what he saw at the power plant.

What happened at the plant?

Nothing happened for a couple of months, but the basement was always creepy to me. That's where the water comes in from the river, and the pipes that carry the water in are just huge—they're like six or eight feet (1.8–2.4 m) in diameter, you know, just huge pipes. I never did like being down there. Even the few times that I worked in the daytime, I did not like to go down there. I avoided it. I just got the feeling like I wasn't wanted down there. I knew it had the potential to be trouble.

It was a lonesome place on the graveyard shift, from 11 p.m. until 7 a.m. Nobody there but me and, sometimes, my little dog, Rastus. But it wasn't really scary, either. It was spotlessly clean and well-lit, there were no cobwebs or dark corners, and best of all, it was easy!

That night that it all happened, I didn't take my dog. I was totally alone, and I was sitting there behind the desk reading a book, and I knew in my gut that something was fixin' to happen. And then the doors on the cabinets out in the hallway fell off and that didn't help me any. [*Laughs.*]

Were the doors loose or something?

They were attached by hinges. Let me give you a little idea of what we're talking about here. In the hallway you stood at this panel, it was like a table about waist high and you had your levers there to control the water filters. If you're standing at the control panel, there are windows and you could look out and watch what the filters were doing. You turn these levers to turn the filters on and off, adjust the depth of the water, and all that. Under the control panel, and facing the hallway, there was just two regular cabinet doors on hinges. They were solid on there, they just didn't fall off—but they did that night.

It was three o'clock in the morning, and I was sitting behind the desk reading a book. Now in the office I was sitting in, the door across from me that went to the hallway was gone. So I was behind the desk and facing that open door to the hallway. And if you went down that hallway and turned to the right, you came to the door that went to the basement. So I'm sitting there behind the desk and I get this creepy feeling that something is not right—something is about to happen. This thing, I don't even really know what to call it, it's the only spirit of this type that I have ever seen and I don't want to see another one. This thing was just totally evil…it was just evil. And the fear that it generated in me…I'm serious when I say I thought I was going to die. I thought my heart was just going to burst.

I knew something was coming, but I didn't know what. Then it drifted into view. It was kind of bouncing just a few inches above the floor and it was going from my right to left. It came from the direction of the basement going down the hall, and when it got centered in that doorway, it turned to face me and it didn't have any features. It had a torso, arms and legs and feet, but no details.

Could you see through it? Was it solid?

No, I could not see through it. It was like a man who had been dipped in tar. But at the same time, since it was floating, I knew that he didn't have any mass—it was a spirit. It was not touching the floor, but it appeared to be solid. It drifted up right to the threshold of the door and it started reaching for me…I'm making the motions now while I'm talking to you, I don't know why…it was reaching its arms out for me, and I figured it was just going to get me because I couldn't move. I froze in my chair. But for some reason it did not come through the door. It started reaching for me, and every time it would reach, its arms would get longer.

I thought I was gone. I was feeling waves of bad energy. Every time it would lean forward and reach for me, the feelings would go all through me.

Was it a feeling of sadness, fear?

Fear, evil, hate, all the negative things you can think of.

Did you feel like it was directed toward you, or it was just making you feel that way?

It was directed toward me. It was an attack.

How did it end?

It made a lunge toward me, and it would straighten back up, and the last time it lunged, it turned like something back down the hall had gotten its attention, or like it heard something. It's hard to say, but it's like something got its attention in the direction that it had come from. It turned and looked back down the hall—he didn't have any eyes, but it turned its head that way. It turned to face me again, and then it turned its whole body and went back in the direction it came from. It was several seconds before I could even breathe, I was just trying to breathe. It had scared me so bad that my whole body was frozen. When I finally caught a big breath—*huhhhhhhh*—it was like it would have been if you were drowning and then finally come up to the top and you take that big breath. I didn't know what to do.

They didn't teach you that during training, huh?

No. [*Laughs.*] It was not in my job description. The first thing I did, I grabbed the telephone. I didn't come out from behind the desk; I grabbed the telephone just to talk to somebody, to know that there was still somebody that I could reach out to. I didn't dare leave. I mean, that was my job. I don't know if I felt a sense of responsibility or fear of being unemployed, but you have to remember it was an important job because I kept the water tanks filled, filtered the water, and then pumped the filtered water to the water tanks which supplied the whole town. It was a fairly responsible position and I didn't dare leave, but I didn't want to stay there either. The rest of the night I would not leave that office. I just let the filters go. I didn't know if that thing was gone or not. I didn't go back out there after that night.

Have you ever talked to anyone else who has worked there?

Oh yeah. Nobody else has seen it, but the last time I talked to anybody who worked there, they said they weren't comfortable there at night, and they carry guns. They're scared, but they don't know what they're scared of. But I do. And I didn't tell them what I saw. But I asked them if they ever got nervous out there, and they said, "Yeah, we get scared out there, that's why we carry guns." But they might as well be carrying slingshots for all that matters.

The water plant is on a hilltop, and there is a small, private nursing facility on the next little hilltop behind the plant. You've gotta be in east Tennessee to know how the hills kind of roll. I had a friend that worked at the little nursing home—you could actually go out the back door of the nursing home and see the water plant. I went up there once and visited with her, and I asked her if anything weird has ever happened. People die in those places— I guess that was more of what I was shooting for—but she said, "Over at that water plant, we hear screams over there at night." And I said, "Really?"

I found out since then that a lot of times with underground water sources, spirits seem to be attracted to them or travel through them or something. I just wonder if that had something to do with it, because it came from the basement where the water comes in.

What do you think you saw that night?

I called it demonic for a long time because I didn't know anything else to call it. If it wanted to hurt me or kill me, I think it could have. But looking back on it, I think it just wanted to scare me. I've read theories, and people say that fear kind of feeds these things. If that's true, and I don't know if it is or not, but if that's true, it sure got a good meal that night.

William Zastrow
Austin, Texas
May 1996

In May of 1996, William Zastrow was 31 years old and driving a delivery truck for a national snack-food company. The shifts were long and the road can make anyone weary when you're on the go all day long. William had an encounter on the road in Austin, Texas, that he believes saved his life.

What time of day did this happen?

It was actually late afternoon, about rush hour, and I was headed back toward the office.

At the time we pulled a lot of long hours. Fourteen- to 16-hour days were common, and that was six days a week. I was headed back to the office after a long day, I didn't realize how tired I was, and I started to doze off.

123

I was coming through downtown Austin; I would say it was well past the capital, probably three quarters of the way past the city. IH 35 is a highway that cuts right through the middle of downtown. I was past the majority of the University of Texas, and there's an area where we have an upper and lower deck on the highway there. I was on the lower level and was heading south because that's where the office was, and I just fell asleep without realizing it.

I fell asleep, and it was at a point where I was at a cemetery that was on the side of the road—right at the edge of the highway. I don't know the name of the cemetery, but the monuments and everything that were there were very ornate. They were larger than what I'm used to seeing. I tried to research to see what the cemetery might've been called. I understand there's supposed to be a state cemetery in that area, but I don't know for sure if that's the one. Anyways, I fell asleep and I couldn't have been asleep more than a few seconds, and something just woke me up. I woke up and instead of looking forward and grabbing the wheel and paying attention to what was doing, I woke up and stared at where a passenger would normally be—so, to my right. I can't explain it. I knew somebody or something was there. I just snapped my head up, looked over, and I could see a shadow. I couldn't make out depth, like if it was 3D or anything like that. It was just a shadow outline, and what struck me about it was I noticed the hair seemed to be short spikes, and I immediately thought it was a young person, a young man.

This shadow was just facing and staring forward and had one hand up under what would be a chin, and was just intent staring forward, and I finally caught on. *I* should be looking forward, and I did.

This was rush-hour time and traffic was stopped. In that area of Austin, it's a very dodgy stretch of highway. There are on-ramps that are literally 30 feet (9 m) [long], so you really have to pay attention. What I did was pretty stupid, but to do it there just increased the risk exponentially.

So I look forward and in my lane there's a dump truck just sitting there. I had to stomp on the brake. I stood up on it, put as much pressure as I could, and at this point I realized from the corner of my eye that we were running out of tombstones—we were coming to the end of the cemetery. And I don't know why I noticed that, I just did. On my left side was the cemetery and next to me was the shadow, and we ran out of tombstones and at that point the shadow seemed to get pulled back—not all at once, it was like he got pulled back in streaks. Realize this was from the side of my eye I was looking at this and taking it all in and watching the dump truck come closer and closer. I finally realized that I wasn't going to stop in time, so I cut a sharp turn in the wheel and went into what I would describe as an emergency lane but it was little more than extra space on the side of the highway. There were concrete barriers to keep cars from going off the road, so it was literally just a little extra room, and I stopped almost equal to the passenger side of the dump truck.

Did you hit anything?

I didn't hit anything, no. It was definitely quite a scare. I didn't feel fear from what I thought I saw next to me. It was the whole incident of: you almost just killed yourself. I definitely came away thinking that whatever was with me saved me that day. I believe it woke me up, and that's what I can't explain. When I woke up, I was no longer groggy. I'm sure some of that might've been the shock of realizing I'd fallen asleep, but I woke up clear as a bell and staring to my right.

Have you been back to the area since?

No, I haven't. My time in Texas was up. I was there for less than a year, and about two weeks after that I had left the company.

Were you a believer in the supernatural before this happened? And are you a believer now?

Not really. I am now, but I don't know how to explain that either. I believe what I've seen, but if someone were to tell me what happened, I would probably scratch my head and wonder: Did that really happen?

But it happened to you.

Yes.

That makes a difference, doesn't it?

Right.

Did this experience change your life?

I'm not sure it really did anything to change my life, other than it was the turning point as far as I really needed to start taking the possibility that there's something else out there seriously. Because I can't really say that it's done anything to dramatically influence my life.

A short while after William and I spoke, he sent me an e-mail:

"I'm sorry to bring this up, but my answer to a question you posed really bothered me. You asked how the experience changed my life. I thought it hadn't, but I realize it allowed me to continue living it."

Jennifer Neighbor
Savannah, Georgia
Fall 2001

Back in 1999, Jennifer Neighbor moved from her home in Ohio to the warmer climes of Savannah, Georgia. After moving, she found employment at the River Street Inn. The building, which used to be a cotton warehouse, was constructed in 1817 and still retains its charm from the bygone era. According to Jennifer, the decor isn't the only relic from the past. One afternoon, she encountered a man whose existence she cannot explain. The 30-year-old assistant food manager also says she's not the only employee to have experienced the unexplained at the Inn.

What brought you to the River Street Inn?

My mom was the operations manager of the hotel, and they needed somebody to do the wine reception. We have a wine reception for hotel guests from 5 p.m. to 7 p.m., six nights a week, and as soon as I moved to Savannah I first started doing that.

I guess it was probably four, maybe five years ago when we opened up an actual food and beverage department. We have meeting rooms on the second floor of the hotel. It's really pretty; there's brick walls—the Savannah red brick—and hardwood floors, that sort of thing. So I started doing that, I guess it was about five years ago, and I became the assistant food manager.

We have a small department—we can't fit that many people in the meeting rooms or anything—so at the time there were probably two of us working there full-time. There were probably two part-timers: we had a bartender, we had somebody else part-time, that sort of thing.

At the time that I saw the ghost it was actually very odd. It was in the afternoon, and it was a pretty day out. I want to say it was in the fall, but I could be wrong. It was just a really pretty day and my manager, Larry, had left to go to the grocery store.

There's actually two entrances into the hallway and into the whole section where I work. There's one that goes out to the atrium, and then there's one that goes out onto a porch. We keep those doors locked because the bar is really only open from 5 p.m. to 7 p.m. unless we have meetings—the entire section will be open for meetings, events, and whatnot. But at that time there was nobody there.

I was setting up for a meeting for the next day. There's three rooms along a long, hardwood-floored hallway, and the Lyman Hall room was the name of the room that I was in. I was setting up pads of paper and pens, and glasses and stuff at each spot, and I was actually facing out toward the hallway when I heard somebody walking by. I looked up and I saw him walk by. I only remember hearing maybe two or three steps before I saw this person walk past the door. And when he walked past, he almost…it's like he almost regarded me. I don't know if he looked at me, but I kind of glanced up and I saw a guy in khaki pants, it looked like tan pants, a white shirt, and what I can best describe as a derby hat. You know the hat with the rim that comes up? He was a Caucasian man with kind of blondish-brown hair. My first thought was that it was my boss.

There were three more footsteps after he passed the doorway, and then the footsteps stopped. I kind of said something, like joking, because I thought it was my boss, but I didn't get an answer. So I thought, it was a guest. I'm like, "Can I help you?" And I didn't hear anything. And I knew they had to be right on the other side of that door. I said, "Can I help you?" again a little louder.

I walked out in the hallway, and there was nobody there. My first thought, you know, being rational, was that one of the doors was unlocked. So I went and checked both of the doors, and both of the doors were locked. I thought if there was anybody in here I would've heard them leave, so I went and checked all the meeting rooms, the bathrooms, I was in the guys' bathroom, I was everywhere, and there was nobody in there. It was bizarre.

When you realized all of the doors were locked and that person was nowhere to be seen, what did you do?

My mom was working up at the front desk at the time, so I ran to the phone and called her, freaking out. I'm like, "Mom, I just saw a ghost. I'm going to sit on the porch." [*Laughs.*] I went and sat on the porch, she came down, unlocked the door and let herself in, and her and a couple of our employees started laughing at me. I wouldn't go back in until my boss got back. [*Laughs.*] He came back and found me sitting on the porch.

We've all had experiences with the lights going on and off, and the TVs. There's two TVs in our billiard room. If the TV goes on or off it's kind of unusual, but it could be explainable unless both of them turn on. I think that's a little odd.

Has that happened, where both turn on?

Yeah. Yeah, we've had that happen. We had a bartender, she died about a year ago—she had an aneurysm and died. When I told her about the ghost, she said, "I've seen him." She explained, and it sounded like this person, but she said he wasn't wearing a hat, so I don't know. I just don't know.

But you saw it too.

Yeah…yeah, I did. And one of the other girls that did the night turndown claimed to have seen him on the fifth floor, or somebody that fit the same description on the fifth floor of the hotel. She does turndown, she puts chocolates and stuff on the beds. Some of the doors you have to kind of turn around and pull to shut them behind you because it's an old hotel, and she claimed she had gone into a room, she had done the turndown, she left the room, went to pull the door shut, and she said there was a guy reaching for the door. She described him and it sounded a lot like the same gentleman.

Have you experienced this person since?

Nope, that was the only time. I haven't seen anything. Really, nobody has; it's kind of odd. The bartender that died last October, she was the last person who said she saw him, and that was a couple years ago. Occasionally you do walk through the cold spots and that sort of thing, and sometimes you hear things and you get creeped out. Like you hear your name being called or something like that when there's nobody there. But besides that, I haven't actually seen him.

Are you ever afraid to be there alone?

Oh yes. I try to not think about it. Sometimes you just get a feeling. You feel like somebody is watching you, or that somebody is in a room. I try not to think about it because I'm there late, but there are times when I've walked down the hallway in front of the billiard room where there's a giant window, and for some reason right there I get chills. I don't know why. I've never seen anything there, but I've heard other people comment on it.

It was really weird when I saw the ghost. I was scared afterward, but I freaked myself out. There wasn't really anything scary about it, except I just freaked myself out. A lot of my friends are like, you're crazy, but I swear I'm not.

Does it bother you to work in a haunted place?

Not really. I've never heard of a ghost killing anybody. [*Laughs.*] If I thought I was in danger…it makes me a little uncomfortable sometimes just when I'm there, and it's late, and I'm tired, and kind of weary, and everything is real quiet. I get that uncomfortable sensation, but it doesn't really scare me. I think it's interesting. I wish I knew exactly what ghosts were.

Michael K. Mather
Horton Grand Hotel, San Diego, California
2002

"Hellooooo," Michael Mather almost sings as hotel guests approach the front desk of the Horton Grand Hotel in San Diego. Mather has worked at the hotel since 1990, and serves as the front office manager. The hotel has a haunted reputation, and Mather talked about his own encounter with two of the resident specters.

Built in 1886, the original section of the Horton Grand has high ceilings and cream-colored wainscoting wood paneling along the lower portion of the walls. Though the owners were careful to match the proportions and style of the older section, when they added a major addition in the 1980s, one can still see where old meets new.

When did you have your experience here?

It was a year or two ago. It was midnight, it just happened to be midnight...I don't know. So I came up to the third floor; I don't get into this that much because not everybody really wants to hear it. I get off the elevator to go and punch out—the offices are up there.

The house was full. There was somebody in every room that night, and I came out of this little vestibule. When the house is full, you can usually hear people in their rooms doing things, but there was no noise, no ambient noise whatsoever. And the halls are not air-conditioned, there's no central air-conditioning in the hall, and the windows are sealed.

131

As I come around the corner, I notice that these curtains are blowing. At that time there were curtains rods above the window, and the curtains went down to below the windowsill. So that's, what? Seven feet (2 m) of curtains? They were all blowing all the way down the hall. I turned and I saw two ethereal little figures scoot around the corner at the end. And I thought, "What was that?" And the curtains were blowing.

Do you have any thoughts on who the two figures may have been?

Probably Harry and Gus. There's the legend of [*the ghosts of children*] Harry and Gus that they died of the fever somewhere along the line.

In the hotel?

I don't know. Some of these things are legends. What was really weird was that about two years later, one of the clerks came down and told me the same story, and I don't think I had told her about what happened to me. So I thought that was kind of odd. Apparently this must happen on a regular basis, but people don't realize it.

The clerk's name was Martha. She came down and she looked kind of white. I said, "What happened?" [*whispers*]. And she told the same story.

Here's the bizarre part. Here is why I think the spirits—if there are any spirits—are attached to the land and not the hotels themselves. Because from right there—that's the original side of the hotel, and this has all been added [*he points to the line between the old and new sections of the building*]. All of this is new. And here is where I saw Harry and Gus scoot around. I don't know where they went; I wasn't going to chase them. And this is all new up to here. Since where I saw them wasn't even part of the hotel originally, I figured it must be associated with the land.

What's one of the more unusual ghost encounters one of the guests has told you about?

I had a guy call down…I mean he had been drinking…and he said [*he makes a drunken voice*], "My pictures are spinning."

What I think is peculiar about my story is that Martha came down and told me the same thing happened to her.

Connie Cook
Palace Station Hotel, Las Vegas, Nevada
September 2004

Buildings don't have to be centuries old or located on historic sites to have ghosts. Built in 1979 (and remodeled twice since), the Palace Station Hotel sits within view of the Las Vegas strip, with only Interstate 15 and the backs of some of the more famous hotels in-between. The hotel has more than 1,000 guest rooms, thousands of square feet of casino gaming, and, according to some of the staff, a ghost who wanders the service area near the hotel conference rooms.

Connie Cook is a 42-year-old bartender and food server who has lived in Las Vegas since she relocated from South Dakota back in 1986.

When did you first hear that the Palace Station Hotel may have a ghost?

When I first started working here, I heard stories. Just stories. There were people that felt a presence—doors would be open when they were locked and supposed to be closed, lights turned on, things moved around, stuff like that.

When did you have your encounter?

It would have been sometime in September of 2004. I got off really late at night. I had worked, like, 18 hours that day. I was dead tired and it was two o'clock in the morning. I was in the back storeroom and I was doing the inventory for the bar, which we have to do every night. While I was back there, I felt something. I looked up and I had seen something like bright white smoke. It wasn't really a form; it looked like a huge cotton ball. It felt like it was kind of looking at me, but I didn't register what it was. I'm thinking, "What the heck is that?" But you know, I'm tired. So it was just done and over. I did my stuff, and I went home.

A month and a half later, I was in the back storeroom putting my bar stuff away again, and I was leaning up against something that was about chest-high. I was writing and this thing walked past me, but this time it was in the form of a human. But again I saw the white smoke. You could see the head and it was moving its arms, but it was gliding. It wasn't, like, walking, but I could tell it had legs.

You call it "it." Do you think it was a man or woman?

I get the impression it was a man, but I don't know that. I could just tell that it had a head and arms; you could tell it was walking. It was moving pretty fast, but I saw it, and I know what I saw. And that's when it registered that it was what I saw a month and a half before—it was the same thing, but it was a different shape.

Have other people talked about seeing this form here?

Yeah. Scott, my partner. He's a bartender that comes up here. He doesn't work a whole lot, but once in awhile. He's seen it twice. But he saw an actual human form. It was a man when he had seen it. Scott told me he was leaning against the bar doing his stuff one night, and he was the only one around. He looked over and this guy was standing right next to him. Scott said it startled him so much that he jumped, and then the man just disappeared. But the other time he'd seen it was back where I had seen it in the store-room. It came walking through the same path that I had seen it take.

Do you have any idea who might be haunting this area, or why?

We have no idea. Maybe a construction worker, maybe some customer still hanging around—we have no idea. There's other porters and stuff who have shut the doors up here and they come walking back by and everything is open.

Are you ever afraid working here because of your resident ghost?

No. Not really, but it is startling sometimes. It doesn't really scare me—it just freaks me out a little bit.

Bobby Mackey
Bobby Mackey's Music World
Wilder, Kentucky

Bobby Mackey is a 57-year-old country singer who has been a musician his entire life. On September 8, 1978, he leased a large, vacant, and dusty building that sits in a small town across the river from Cincinnati, Ohio—a building that had quite a past. The structure was built in the 1850s and originally served as a slaughterhouse. After prohibition ended in 1933, the building became a tavern and casino. The ownership changed hands several times over the next few decades and the tavern had various names, but stories of gambling, police raids, and murder clung to the location.

The most famous ghost said to be haunting the building is that of Johanna. The legend is that Johanna was the daughter of a former club owner and she fell in love with one of the singers who was a regular performer there. She became pregnant by the entertainer, and in a rage, her father had the singer killed. Johanna was so upset at the loss that she tried to poison her father and then took her own life.

By the time Mackey moved into the building in 1978, the days of clandestine gambling and shoot-outs were gone. But the ghostly legends were not. Johanna's story was enough to inspire Bobby to immortalize her story in song on one of his recent albums. Today, Bobby Mackey's Music World is one of America's best-known haunted locations, even though its owner and namesake has neither seen nor believes in ghosts.

Did you hear about the ghostly legends when you bought the building?

No. No, I didn't. My wife and I and some other people were in there, and we are ready to make the deal on the lease, and there was an option to buy it. This guy up the street…this kid…he was a kid at the time, barely 18 or 19, comes walking in and he said, "Hi, I'm Carl. I know everything about the place if you need any help or anything."

Well, yeah, we needed help. So we talked to him. We told him we needed the place cleaned up and we needed some painting done, and this, that, and the other. He knew where everything was, all the switches—it's a big place and it was like there were hidden rooms and everything, and Carl knew everything about it.

My wife was pregnant at the time, and as a few days and weeks went by, Carl started telling her about this ghost stuff and he had her attention. He tried to tell it to me, and I wouldn't listen. I told him I didn't want to hear any of that stuff. Because I didn't believe it then. I don't believe now.

So you don't believe in ghosts now, but certainly there's been customers and staff throughout the years who have told you about their various experiences. What do you think is going on?

Through the years, mostly employees have told me this or that happened. I'm just not one to dwell on it. I look at the big picture. I'm into lots of things…my music, mainly. I always figured there's got to be an explanation. But I do have to say that a lot of the people who have told me these things, I have a lot of respect for.

So you don't think they're lying.

No. I don't see it as they're lying or making it up. I don't know if they're taken in by the stories, but they mean well, and they believe what they say.

How do you think the legend about your ghosts grew so big?

Doug Hensley, who wrote the book *Hell's Gate*, he had a movie rental store and he asked me to do a TV commercial for him. I went over one Friday morning to film his commercial. [After filming] the commercial, the sales rep from the TV station was a good friend of both of ours and so we went back in Doug's office at his store, and Doug started reading some things he had written. He was real proud of this fiction novel he was writing—it was real gory and stuff, and it reminded me of stuff Carl had been trying to tell me about my club.

I told Doug that, according to Carl, there's a story about the club that's for real. I said, "You're writing this fiction. There's a story over the club that's based on reality. So that got his interest and that night he came over to the club and tried to approach Carl. And I told Carl many times to keep it to himself because I didn't want to hear that stuff. I told him not to be telling anybody. So Carl wouldn't talk to Doug.

During the night I'd be on stage singing, I was busy, and Doug came to me and said, "Carl won't talk to me." I said, "Well, I told him not to." Finally, later in the night Doug got Carl with me and at that point I threw my hands up and I said, "Carl, you've been trying to tell me this stuff for years. If you want to tell it, go and tell him."

In the back of my mind, I didn't really think that Doug would follow through with it. But he did. [*Laughs.*] He just got obsessed with it. Doug would call me, and he would talk to Carl, and he made notes, and he wrote this book. That's how it came about, and it got to a point where I couldn't stop it if I wanted to.

What about your song "Johanna"? At what point do your ghosts make it into your music?

I had some ties in Nashville. I was in Nashville doing a lot of things, and I was there quite often. I had a partner there, and we had a recording studio together. He's very sharp, he's written a lot of songs and stuff, and I made mention to him about the stories at the club. We had been doing some recording and we were kind of wrapping up, and he was sitting there on the piano stool and I had told him a little bit about it. He said, "What year was all this?" It was the heyday of the old gambling casino, you know? I said, "Back in the 30s, 40s." He just strummed his guitar and he said the opening line, saying, "Way back in the thirties, in the little town of Wilder..." and it went from there. He and I ended up writing the song in about 20, 25 minutes.

So, life and ghosts inspiring art.

He didn't know the story, but as I fed it to him, we put the lyrics together.

Is that song a hit in your club?

Yeah. People don't dance to it much, so I kind of stay away from it in that respect. But it's been a hit there. But my music has many boundaries. Everybody wants to know, "You don't believe in it, but you wrote this song…." I said, "Well, it fit the story."

Have the ghosts been good for business?

It hasn't hurt. I prefer being known for a great country music place and a great dance place. Some people are fascinated with the mystique of the ghosts, but the majority of people I don't think pay any attention to it anymore.

(*Author's aside*) "Johanna, Johanna, where are you now? Could it be you're still here somehow?"—*from the title*

Chapter 4

Haunted Hotels and Inns

Photo source: © istockphoto.com/Kevin Russ

Inns and hotels are transient places by design. People come and go for a myriad of different reasons—some happy, some sad. When we rent a room, our minimum expectations are usually cleanliness and privacy. But because the hotel room isn't home, our senses are a bit heightened to the noises, smells, sights, and other nuances of the building. Though privacy is promised by those who offer lodging, it can't always be delivered when ghosts are present.

Some hotels are built into and around historic locations—places that weren't always made for lodgers. In some cases, the spirits haunting the guest rooms and halls have come from a bygone era. But in a few cases, the presence of an entity can't be explained by any study of history.

Jaci Burkett
The Farnsworth House Inn, Gettysburg, Pennsylvania
July 25–27, 2003

Jaci Burkett and her mother are both Civil War reenactors, and at least once a year they make the trip from their western Pennsylvania home to Gettysburg. "For me it's just the most interesting time period," said 17-year-old Jaci. "I feel a real connection to the Civil War. I've had so many ghost experiences at Gettysburg; it's my favorite place to be."

In Gettysburg, a place where ghost lore lurks around every tree and in almost every building, one location seems to have more than its share of ghosts: The Farnsworth House Inn. In July of 2003, Burkett and her mom made their reservations at the Farnsworth to check out the ghosts for themselves. They had more than a few supernatural experiences while staying there.

What did you think of the inn when you arrived?

We arrived around noon. We checked in at the bookstore, which is where you're supposed to check in, and the woman took us up to our room—the Schultz Room. It was such a beautiful room. She put the key in the lock, and when she tried to turn it, it would turn back all by itself. She kept trying to do that several times, and each time the lock did that. She said, "Oh, it looks like you have a visitor." And she said not to worry—they just like to play tricks.

At that point I kept telling myself, "I'm not going to be afraid. Ghosts don't exist." And then when that happened with the lock, I started to get a little bit scared. She opens up the door and there's nothing there. No breeze, no change in temperature or anything. She gave us the key and she said, "Go ahead and have a look around if you want." So we put our stuff in the room and we decided to explore the house.

We were on the second story and we walked upstairs to the attic, which was called the Garret Room. It had once been a room that people could sleep in, but it had so much activity that they had actually locked it, and the only time they unlock it is whenever they give ghost tours. So my mother and I walked up the stairs and there was a heavy padlock on the door, and as soon as we reached the door, the lock started shaking and then all of a sudden, it stopped and some invisible force—it felt like a wind—just blew down the stairs and it brushed past my mom and it brushed past me. We tried to look through the cracks of the door to see if there was a fan or something in there, and there was a fan, but it was turned off. So I was freaked out.

How was your mom holding up at that point?

She thought it was amazing. My mom's tough.

So we explored the house for a little bit longer, and when we went back to our room, I opened the door, I walked forward, and the bed was completely messed up. The sheets looked like somebody had been sleeping on them, and there was an indentation in the pillows. I was so shocked I couldn't even speak. I just gasped, and my mom said, "What is it? What is it?" We had just walked into the room—we were sure no one else would have had access to it—and we noticed the bed. So we made up the bed and we decided to try it again. We went outside our room, we closed the door, and we waited there for maybe five minutes or so, and we walked back in and it happened again. It's like somebody had been sleeping in the bed.

While you were standing right outside the door?

We were right outside the door, and we didn't hear any footsteps, we didn't hear any sounds—we just walked back inside and the bed was messed up again.

Later on, we went to bed, maybe around 11 o'clock, and around five o'clock in the morning, we heard the lock on the door being messed with. Our first thought was that somebody's trying to get into the room, so we sat up and just looked at the door. The door unlocked. It was a deadbolt and it unlocked, and the door opened up slowly all by itself. We looked out into the hall, but there was nobody there. No shadows or anything, and then the door closed again and it locked all by itself. My mom and I were like, "This is so amazing."

That was the main door to your room?

The main door, and the only door.

Earlier that night, my mom had moved several cat statues—they were the ugliest statues. [*Laughs.*] She moved them off of these two antique chairs, and she said, "If there's any spirits here, you're welcome to sit down, you're welcome to stay." I just laughed. I thought she sounded ridiculous. But that night, you could hear creaking like somebody was squirming, sitting down in them, and trying to get comfortable. But I couldn't see anybody and neither could my mother. I said, "Oh my gosh, it worked."

We were only allowed to stay in the Schultz Room for one night because there was a cancellation. So the next day, we had to move our stuff into the Eisenhower Room in the newer part of the inn.

The next evening around 8 p.m. or so, we went to the Farnsworth House basement for ghost stories. It was a nice half-hour show and they tell you ghost stories, some legends, and some history about the house. Supposedly there are 14 spirits in that house, but not all from the Civil War era.

After the show, we went up and we told the woman who was telling the stories about what happened the night before with the door opening and the chair, and she said, "Oh yes, so you're the people who were staying in that room." And we were a little bit confused. We said, "Yeah, why?" She said, "That was the soldier sitting down, and he wanted me to tell you that he was thanking you for letting him stay and rest." We were like, "Oh my gosh." Because we never told her that we said, "You can stay and rest here, please sit down," or whatever, and she knew about it. And then she said, "Whenever the door opened, that was the soldier letting you know that he had rested, and that was him leaving the room."

145

Later that night, we went back to the Eisenhower Room, and I showered around 11 p.m., then my mom went and she got her shower. I was just sitting on the bed writing, and all of a sudden there's pressure beside me on the bed. I looked over and there was another indentation on the bed, like somebody was sitting down. Well, I screamed, I ran into the bathroom, and I said, "Mom! Mom! Someone just sat on the bed." My mom came running out and when we came back out, there was a little two- or three-inch (5–8 cm) white feather laying on the bed. I don't know where it came from. I figured maybe it was from the pillow or something; I didn't have anything that had feathers on it. I still have that feather.

Burkett was told by employees of the inn that the pillows don't have feathers in them because of Pennsylvania hotel requirements.

We went back to the room, and we went to bed a little bit later that night. During the night, I kicked off all of the covers because it got so hot. I said, "Mom, I'm just so hot, I can't sleep." My mom said, "Oh, that feels nice." I said, "What feels nice?" She said, "You're playing with my hair." I said, "I'm not playing with your hair." She was half-in and half-out of sleep, and she's like, "Well, it still feels nice." [*Laughs.*]

I was clutching the mattress because I was so scared. I tried to drift back off to sleep, and then the covers were pulled back on over me. I take them off again and I said, "Stop it," but my mom didn't reply. I just tried to fall asleep again, and again the covers were pulled over me and someone pinched my arm. I kicked them off and I got kind of snippy with my mom. I said, "Mom, stop covering me up, I'm too hot." She said, "I didn't cover you up. I'm trying to sleep here." I was terrified. And the pinches felt like someone was trying to make the point like, "Stop, this is for your own good."

We went back to sleep and I decide to keep the covers on and hold onto them for dear life. Several hours later, my mom wakes me up, she's pushing me, and she goes, "Mary! Mary, Jaci, there's Mary!" Mary was one of the spirits who was a midwife at the house. I said, "Where is she? I don't see her." My mom is pointing frantically going, "Right there. She's right there. How can you not see her?" And I said, "Well, I just can't see her. I don't know." I was looking and my mom was pointing around the room like Mary was moving, and then my mom pointed to the wall like she just went through the wall. I said, "Is she still here?" And my mom said, "No, she just went through the wall. But I could see her face. She had wrinkles and her hair was braided. I could see the collar of her dress, but I couldn't see anything past her torso." I figured maybe Mary realized me being a kid, like I was scared and she can only appear to certain people and she doesn't want to scare me.

I thought that weekend was so amazing, and ever since then we've been going back to the Farnsworth every year.

Have you had any experiences since?

Oh, yes. Definitely. There's been reports of two spirit children in the inn. On another trip to the Farnsworth, my mom and I were very tired and we went to bed maybe around 10 o'clock. Several minutes later, we started hearing kids running up and down the stairs and back and forth in the hall. We said, "You know, if they don't stop within the next five minutes, we're going to get up and ask them to please be quiet, or go to bed, tell their parents or something." So the running went on and on and on. They'd run down the hall, run back to where our door was, and then the sounds stopped outside our door. And you'd hear giggles and then they started running down the stairs. Then the running would start from a different place, they wouldn't be coming from downstairs, they'd be coming from the upstairs and running back to our room, and then back downstairs. We had had enough. My mom went and she waited by the door, ready to open it up the next time the kids came over. Whenever they ran past, you did see shadows, you could see the shadows at the bottom of the door. So my mom waited until she could hear them coming again and when they were coming down the hall, she opened up the door, but there was no one there. No shadows, nothing. It was so freaky.

Jaci and her mom have gone back to the Farnsworth each year. They have since brought recording equipment and cameras, turning their stay into a bit of a ghost hunt as well.

Tom Haikin
Breadsall Priory, Derby, England
October 2004

Tom Haikin is a 56-year-old man from Tehachapi, California, who works for a company that designs and installs aircraft modifications—a business that has him meeting with prospective clients all over the world to negotiate contracts and discuss needs. One such business trip had Haikin traveling to Derby, England, and staying at the Marriott hotel at Breadsall Priory, where he encountered all three of the ghosts said to be haunting the building.

What was the Breadsall Priory like?

When I pulled up in the driveway and I see the sign that says, "Watch for ghosts," I say, "It's a Marriott, gimme a break…it's gotta be bogus." I knew there were a lot of stories in the town of

Derby itself, which was an industrial town. There were a lot of stories about children being put to work and getting injured or killed, so there were lots of ghosts in the town, but I didn't know anything about the Breadsall Priory other than it had been owned

The Breadsall Priory in Derby, England.
Photo by Edd Dumbill

by a number of people and it was now a hotel.

How did you end up at that hotel?

I went on a business trip. There were about five of us, and our function was to get together with the customer and try to work out the details of the trip. So it had nothing to do with ghosts whatsoever. In fact, I have no idea to this day why the big muckitymuck said, "Let's go to the Breadsall Priory," because it was not convenient as far as being a place where you can do business. It didn't have online DSL; you had to use a dial-up modem. It didn't have any office space where you could do work. It just had two 18-hole golf courses, but nobody brought clubs. So we just happened to be there—it was the place he thought he wanted to go.

The place was originally built as a small area and then it got bigger, and they added on, and added on, and the add-ons don't exactly match up real well. Once I was there, I found they had literature about the ghosts, so I got curious. One day, when I had a little bit of extra time, I went into the front section, which is the main section of the building that was built in 1250. I walked up these little tiny stairs, I get up into this hallway, and it's kind of odd. The doors are so small, I said, "I don't know if I can get through this." Almost like *Alice Through the Looking Glass*—the doors were too small. I go through the hallway and turn around. I look up, and I'm looking over the doorframe and there's a guy… kind of like a little spirit. I don't see a firm figure. I felt the presence of him, and I knew it was a guy. I knew he was retreating back into the corner, like…"Please…." There was a wedding going on, and people playing golf, and there was all kinds of stuff, and all he really wanted was to be left alone.

What did the man look like?

I did not see facial features—I just sensed the presence. From just being there, I sensed that it was a man, that he was a couple of hundred years old, and that he was a monk, and not necessarily because I was at a priory where the priests lived. I just sensed that it was a monk, and that's what I got. He wasn't a hermit-type monk; he was just overwhelmed by all of the human presences that were around him. And all he wanted to do was hide.

I saw him, and I kind of communicated a quiet: "I'm sorry that you have to go through this." Then I went on about my business.

That night I went to bed early because we were leaving the next day, and I had to get up at four o'clock in the morning to go catch a plane. It was that night that I started having a coughing spell from all of the changing weather and the airplane flight. So the coughing woke me up. I'm sitting up and kind of semi-reclining. The lights are all out, and I hear this noise that sounds like a little mouse or something playing with power cords. I turn the light on a couple of times, but there were no mice in there. I turn the lights off and the noise came back, and so I got the impression—and again, I don't see them, I feel them—and I just knew it was a little boy. I was in the new wing; it's not where the ghosts normally hang out. The ghosts normally hang out in the old section. So I said, "It's your place. Go ahead and look through whatever you want." That's when I heard some noise in my suitcase. I just kind of relaxed and laid back and the noise went away after a while. I tried to get comfortable and I started coughing again, and as I started coughing that's when I felt somebody tucking me in. I sensed the presence of a matronly kind of a woman—I was thinking of the white, blouse-y kind of a top, a scoop-neck kind of a thing—an older woman, probably in her fifties. I was tucked in all on the left side and I said, "Thank you," and I laid down and went to sleep.

The next morning as I went to pack, I opened up my suitcase and there is my little bag of all of those electronic parts—you know, the voltage converters? They were all scattered around the inside of the suitcase, and the night before I had put them away and pulled the little drawstring closed and everything. I think the little boy was satisfied after playing with them. The little boy was like any little boy—he was curious. And the woman was looking out for me.

At this point I still didn't know who the ghosts were. I hadn't spoken to anybody at the hotel. So I went down to check out, and I said to them, "Do you have three ghosts here?" And he said, "Yeah, why?" I said, "Is one of them a monk?" "Yeah." "One of them is a little boy?" "Yeah." "And one of them is a woman?" "Yeah." I picked up on all three of them, and I didn't have any preconceived notion about what it was. They were startled that I found all three because though the monk was in the old section, the two others didn't normally venture into the other section of the hotel. I think I invited them, so they came.

Nora Quick
Albuquerque, New Mexico
February 2001

When Nora Quick was 20 years old, she and her friend, Brooke, set out on a road trip from Chicago, Illinois, to Phoenix, Arizona. Similar to most young people, the two girls were on a tight budget, so choosing overnight lodging usually came down to a matter of cost. One inexpensive motel the two encountered in Albuquerque offered a frightening experience that was more than they bargained for.

Today, Quick is an accounting clerk living in Oregon with her husband.

What brought you to Albuquerque back in February of 2001?

I had an opportunity to go to Phoenix to take a training class, and I was actually offered a job there subsequent to that. So I packed up everything I owned—it fit in a little Geo Prizm—and I took my best friend, and we just hit the road. By the time we got to Albuquerque, it was really late at night—it was almost midnight.

We had gone through the Ozarks that day, and it was just a heck of a drive. Of course, being young, our budget was pretty tight. We kind of eschew the Holiday Inn and all of those other kinds

152

of names, so we took the last exit in Albuquerque and came to the Desert Sands Inn. We thought it was kind of neat because we were sort of following Route 66 and this kind of had that feel to it. So, we thought, this didn't look like a bad place and we stopped in.

The night clerk, I remember him, he was from India and had a very thick accent. He wasn't very easy to talk to. He gave us room 109. It was on the first level in the corner in a building separate from the main building, and it was in clear view of where we could park our car. So for two girls who were 20 and 19, we felt pretty safe. It was well-lit, and that was really what we were looking for. They had good locks, good security measures, lots of light, and that was really the important thing. I also remember it was dirt cheap, which was really good, so we went ahead and came in and got settled down.

We walked in, and Brooke set her bag down on the first bed and I was still walking to mine when the television in the corner came on. We thought that was a little weird. At first we worried that we set a bag down on a remote, and then we realized they didn't have a remote—I guess you have to pay to get them there. I do know sometimes with televisions, people within a certain radius or who have a similar remote can turn it on and off—that's what we thought it was. So we turned it off and then it came on again. We looked out the window trying to see if anybody was screwing around with us, and then the weirdest thing I have ever seen in my life happened.

When you got into the room, did you get an uneasy feeling from it?

After the TV turned on by itself, we did get this feeling like we were being watched. Of course, being girls of that age, we were more thinking that somebody was peeping at us. So we checked the curtains and kind of got a little paranoid, and we started checking for video cameras, checking corners, the sprinkler system, and everything. We really did have the feeling that we were being watched, but we couldn't find anything. That was really the only strange thing we felt at that time.

But the room seemed nice enough otherwise?

The time we were there, there were no signs of any mold or decay, paint chips, or anything. It was a typical middle-America cheap motel. You know that feeling you get from hotel rooms? It's kind of a transitional place. They're not really happy or sad or anything, but we really got the feeling that someone was watching us in that room.

Being in the corner room, we were a little nervous and checked around, but when we didn't find anything we felt okay, and that's when all of a sudden, the TV channels started to go up. It would go to channel two, channel three, channel four, channel five, channel six, channel seven…but at the same time, the volume was going up to the maximum and down to the minimum. I have never in my life seen a television that could do both things at the same time. It was unbelievable. We were just really, really unnerved by then. So we went ahead and unplugged the television and ran out. We couldn't really tell what was going on, so we just went to the car.

My friend Brooke and I were both really logical people and thought that there had to be a very sane, reasonable explanation, so we kind of talked ourselves into thinking we had imagined it. When we came in again, the television was plugged back in—and we had a clear sight of the room the entire time and had not seen anyone go in after us. Then the television came back on and the light started to flicker.

What kind of lights were they? Was it just one light that flickered?

I believe there were two lamps right above the beds, then there was a table lamp over by the television, and then there was a little hallway lamp between the bathroom and the main room, and all of them started flickering at the same time. Not simultaneously; the one would be on and two would be off, then the two would be on and one would be off—it was kind of random. That made us pretty nervous.

My friend, she was always a little bit more logical than I, and she asked if I knew if there would be a Bible in there. We did find a Gideon Bible. She's Jewish, so she started to read some passages from the Old Testament, and the really strange thing is, and I just don't understand this, when she was reading, everything stopped. I thought that was kind of strange.

She got kind of tired, and I'm sort of the braver of the two, and so she asked if I would read. I wasn't really raised in any particular religion, so I was fairly familiar with the Bible, but not particular passages or meanings or anything. When I was reading, I noticed it stopped as well, but it didn't seem to matter where I was reading from. I began to think that it maybe had something more to do with me making noise than what I was reading. If I was reading but I wasn't speaking, it was still going on, but as long as I kept talking, as long as I kept making noise, I noticed it stopped. I found that to be very strange.

After a little while, I felt pretty confident and everything seemed to be okay, so I went ahead and I closed the Bible. I left the lights on and tried to get to sleep, but as soon as I closed my eyes, the television and the lights turned on, and then we heard a sound coming from the bathroom. The only way I can describe this sound is when I was a little kid, I had a next-door neighbor that had an Irish Wolfhound. You know, those are really big dogs and have really full barks and really full snarls. My neighbor's dog had actually gotten bit by a raccoon and it was rabid and they had to put it down. But I remember them chasing it through the neighborhood and the sounds it made. It was the sound of an animal in pain, but also an animal that wanted to hurt. It was really weird to hear an animal expressing those kind of emotions, and that's almost what we heard coming from the bathroom. That was the point at which we cursed at the top of our lungs, grabbed our shoes, unplugged the television again, and ran out and slept in the car. We just weren't going to put up with that.

Of course it's pretty cold there in February, so we made it to the morning by turning the car on and then the sun rose. Everything just feels better in the day. We started to think about ghost movies, and thinking, well, nothing ever happens in the day. We found that was not good logic. [*Laughs.*]

We came back in, and the television was plugged in and on and the clock radio alarm was going, and we hadn't set that at all. So we turned everything off and what we did was, being screwed-up kids that we were, we decided one person could go and shower and clean up and the other person would sit there with the door open. It just made us feel better to have the door open, to be able to see people outside and see cars.

About a minute and a half after Brooke got in the shower, she came out screaming and naked. And she's not a naked kind of person, with a door open and the world outside—that's not her personality at all. And she said that she had set her shampoo bottle down by her knees and it had hit her head. That she had ducked her head under the water and she felt it hit the side of her head. She had a red mark on her forehead. At this point I was pretty much in firm denial, and so I told her, "Well, maybe you were holding it, and you're soapy, and it kind of hit you."

So I decided I would be the big, bad, brave one and go and take my shower. At that point I had really long hair—it was pretty much to my waist. I was in there and I was soaping up, and it's a very distinct feeling: I felt somebody grab my hair, twist it, and then wind it around their wrists. That's a very distinct gesture, and then it yanked back and I actually had some hair ripped out. There was nothing that my hair could've caught on, there were no handles and the shower nozzle wasn't in the right area.

So I felt that and of course I did the same thing Brooke did—I ran out screaming at the top of my lungs. We packed everything we could as fast as we could and got out of Dodge.

Are you a believer now?

Unfortunately, yes. That's something you just can't discount. If that was a person I could see and identify, they'd be in jail.

Chapter 5

Near-Death Experience

Image source: © istockphoto.com/Eva Serrabassa

Most people experience ghosts and spirits when entities cross over from their own world or plane to ours. But a select few of us actually cross in the other direction—going from the world of the living to the world of spirits, and then come back to tell about it. Near-death experiences, or NDEs, are among the most profound of human experiences because not only does the witness have an intense spiritual encounter, they also come back to learn that their physical bodies actually died, if only for a few moments. The evidence is impossible to ignore or discount for the person who goes through the NDE.

Sandra Brooks
Clifton Forge, Virginia
July 1960

Sandra Brooks is a 58-year-old nurse and a mother of three. She has a unique perspective on the afterlife, in that she's already been there. When she was 12 years old, she had an accident that left her without a pulse and unresponsive. Brooks believes she caught a glimpse of the afterlife, and though this happened several decades ago, the details are still quite vivid in her mind. The event has helped shape her life, especially how she deals with her patients who are terminally ill and facing their own mortality.

What was the accident that caused your near-death experience?

I was 12 years old and cousins were visiting. We had decided to go to a local state park called Douthat. It was very hot outside and, of course, being children, we didn't pay any attention to our parents when they said, "Don't go in the water until we get there." And so we went on in the water, and the water was very, very cold. The lake is cold all of the time because it's mountain-fed—we're right in the middle of the mountains; you don't find any warm water around there. And of course it was very hot outside, so I guess it was the change of temperature that affected me.

I don't remember any of this, but I found out later I was on the bottom of the lake looking up. What turned out to be a friend of mine, who I later went to high school with, saw me in the water and went down and brought me out. My mother later told me that I was gray in color at that time. In 1960, they didn't have any kind of telephone on the beach; they didn't have any oxygen or anything like that. They had to run the full length of the beach up to another site and get a telephone to call the rescue squad. At that time they were doing whatever measures they needed to do to me.

They brought me back around—of course I don't remember any of this—and they put me in the ambulance. The ambulance people, who I later became friends with, told me that they had had to do CPR on me two or three times in the ambulance, and when I got to the hospital I was breathing, but when I got into the emergency room I had stopped breathing again. Later in life, I became a nurse and I had talked to the nursing personnel that had taken care of me that day. They told me that I had no blood pressure, pulse, or respiration when I was in the emergency room.

The first time I remember something was sitting in the emergency room watching them work on me, and I thought it was really strange that I could see what they were doing. It was like I was sitting up above everything watching them. Being a 12 year old, I had no idea what was going on.

The second time I remember something was when I saw this light and I was going toward it. I got to the light and that's where I saw my grandfather—I was five when he passed away—and I asked him where I was, and he didn't say, but he told me that he didn't think I was supposed to be there yet. Being a curious 12 year old, I kept saying, "Where am I?" And of course he never answered me. We talked, and it's very hard to describe what I saw. I knew I was in a place that there were tons and tons of different eras of people because there were so many different types of dress. This may sound unusual, but I never saw my grandfather's arms and hands, but I saw his face. But at the same time I felt a hug—he hugged me when I first saw him.

After we talked for a few minutes, he told me he wanted me to meet someone. My grandmother had been standing behind him; my grandfather was a lot taller than she. I was only 18 months old when she passed away, so I really didn't have a recollection of her. I met her and she was a beautiful woman. She had long, black hair and piercing eyes, a very gentle face. Both of them were very happy—that's what I remember.

We talked for a few minutes, and that was when this hand came out of cloud. I never saw anything but this hand and it had scars on it—indentations like nails or something like that—and I had a warm feeling. The hand pointed down, and the next thing I remember I was in a hospital bed. I remember my mother, and I remember people around me, and they wanted to give me a shot and I told them to give it to my mother. [*Laughs.*] I wanted to go back to where I had come from because it was so peaceful and calm, the temperature was just perfect. It was just total...I don't know the word...it was total euphoria.

How old did your grandfather appear to be?

He appeared to be as I remember him when I was five. I've often wondered if that was his way of me being able to recognize who he was. Now my grandmother, she didn't look old, and she didn't look real young. But she didn't have any gray hair. She looked like a middle-aged woman—very healthy, very happy, very glad to see me.

Do you recall seeing a tunnel, or did you just see light?

I don't know if I could describe it as a tunnel; it just seemed like there was a beam of light. It was like the beam was on either side of me, the rays of it, but I was going to the essence of the light.

What do you make of the hand pointing downward?

I've always felt like it was Jesus. I'm a Christian, but I'm not one of these hellfire and damnation people either. But I felt like it was the Lord telling me it wasn't my time. I needed to go back down to where I came from, whether I wanted to or not—I was going. It was just something that was totally out of my control.

I went to church and Sunday school, that type of thing. At 12, even though you go to church and Sunday school, you don't realize what Christianity is like—not like you do when you're an adult.

Given how long it's been since this happened, how has it affected your life?

For a long time I thought I was totally insane for even thinking what had happened had really happened. And I really didn't think a whole lot about it after a while, because I didn't want anybody to know what had happened. [*Laughs.*] Because I thought they might think "this girl's crazier than she really is!"

It really had some significance to me when I went into nursing in the 70s. We were studying death and dying, [*Elisabeth*] Kubler-Ross, and that type of thing, and she started talking about the death experiences that people had who would come back. These people had told her and related all of these things. And I thought, "Hmm,

163

this sounds very familiar to me," so I read up on it just to satisfy myself that I was not really insane for experiencing this.

As a nurse I have dealt with a lot of people who were dying. My experience has given me insight. I can sit down and talk about death without any fear of it. I'm trying to help people who are in that position in life to not have the fear of dying. Maybe the fear of what you're dying from, but not the fear of dying—that it will be a comfortable journey, so to say.

I have three children. They're adults now, and I have told them about this experience. I've told them the actual process of dying, going on and seeing your relatives again, and seeing people who have loved and nurtured you and so forth. That's the good part.

Later in life as my mother got older, and of course I did too, I would talk to her about it. She didn't like to talk about it, but I kept telling her about this experience I had in seeing my grandparents and all of this. I said, "You know, Mom, it wasn't bad." I was trying to make her feel better about the process. When my mother passed away, I was with her and I told her, "Hey Mom, you know how I feel about this dying," and I said, "When you see Daddy, give him a kiss for me." And she said, "Well, he's right here, you do it yourself."

All of my family was there by her bedside, and I didn't think it was eerie for my mom to see my dad. I didn't think it was different because I've been through the death experience. I feel that we have people around us all the time; we just don't realize that they're there and that they are protecting us and helping us through hard times, difficult times. It's just something that we need to accept and realize—that we are not alone.

Being in the medical field, have you had the opportunity to speak with others who have gone through the near-death experience?

I've talked to a lot of people who have had these different experiences. I talked to this one man who had five near-death experiences. He had five heart attacks and he was telling me what he saw, and his were similar circumstances and similar experiences. The majority of people that I have talked to that have had these have all had similar experiences. Except, I did talk to this one lady. I don't know what kind of life she lived, I don't know what kind of circumstances she based her life on, but she said it was the most horrifying feeling that she had ever experienced in her life. She said that she was plunged into a dark hole and it was very frightening. She said she never wanted to experience anything like that again. I said, "Well, I wonder why that happened to you?" I didn't want to be...*nosy*...I guess is the word, into her lifestyle and this type of thing. And she said, "I don't know, but I think I'm going to have to figure this out and change myself." I think she thought she went down to hell.

I think the death experience that I had did open me up, and it made me realize that there are other forces that are around us—and if we just relax and listen, we can learn.

Chapter 6

While You Were Sleeping

Source images: "Pillow" © istockphoto.com/Stacey Walker &
"Old Dead Relative #2" © istockphoto.com/Julie Merchant

Sleeping is a vulnerable state to be in. We're lying down, unconscious, and subject to whatever elements may storm into our bedrooms. Some people have dreams that they feel were "more than a dream," an actual spirit contact. The sleep state may make some second-guess any unexplained phenomena they encounter, either during sleep, or just after waking up. But some experiences are so significant that the witness reminds themselves at the time of the encounter that they're awake and definitely not dreaming. A fear of the dark and of things creeping in the night goes back to our childhoods. For some, their worst fear is to find there really is a monster lurking in the closet.

Jerry E. Spivey
Brooklyn, New York
Circa 1958

Jerry Spivey had a rough start to his young life. He was born premature, and in his first weeks of life doctors told his mother he wasn't going to survive. He says his mother told him that when she began to pray for him, infant Jerry started to smile and then pulled through. His father died when he was young, and his family was broken up. By age six, Jerry had been separated from his mother to stay with his aunt and uncle in Brooklyn, and his brother was sent to live with family in North Carolina. Jerry secluded himself quite a bit during childhood. Around age six, he had a frightening encounter that has been permanently etched into his memory.

Today, Spivey does computer work at a law firm while pursuing his passion of writing and producing music. The former preacher has never forgotten his childhood encounter and how the events affected his direction in life.

Can you take us back to 1958?

It's still very graphic in my head. I didn't play like the other little kids. I used to sit in my little red rocking chair, and I used to rock, and I used to daydream. My aunt raised me, and the doctors told my aunt that they had to take that little red rocking chair away from me. But she told them if you take that little red chair away from him, it's really going to tear him up—he's a little kid, it's going to destroy him. They said she had to come up with an approach to get this chair away from me.

Why were you so attached to the chair?

I had a traumatic childhood. I wasn't with my mother, my father got killed, I wasn't with my brother, and I was being raised by my father's sister. There were times when she was beating me, you know. I was a really troubled child—I was going through a lot. I guess she was trying, though. She was trying to raise me.

It's kind of weird how people can open up this world for other people just by telling them something. My aunt told me, she said, "Jerry, you know something…" She explained to me how I had to get out of that rocking chair—I had to stop rocking in the rocking chair and the whole bit. And of course I didn't. She told me one night, she said, "You know something, one of these nights you're gonna see something in that rocking chair." This was to scare me. And I was like, "Yeah sure, I'm not going to see anything in my rocking chair."

My uncle used to go out and gamble, and he would stay out all night long sometimes. My aunt would come into my room and wake me up and I would come in and sleep with her—that type of thing. I had this little clown, and the clown had this little spike or something on top of his head, like a hat type of thing. On this particular night, I put the clown in the rocking chair, which happened to be in my aunt's room. I don't know if I was rocking in her room that particular day, or what was happening. But I loved that clown and I used to lay the clown down in the rocking chair. It must have been about three o'clock in the morning—and there's no way my aunt did this and no other kid was going to be up at that hour. I went over this a thousand times, but I've had so many ghostly experiences that I realize that what happened next wasn't my aunt. It was a demon, actually, which she summoned.

Around three o'clock in the morning, I wake up. When I woke up, the first thing I could see was my rocking chair by the window, and the moon was reflecting in and there was a flower that was on the windowsill, and on the chair was my clown. I'm looking at my clown and I'm noticing that my rocking chair and my clown are rocking, and not only are they rocking, but the clown is playing with the flower that was on the windowsill. I'm a kid, and my aunt is dead asleep. You know how you wipe your eyes? What is this? What is going on here? And I'm looking at this thing and it's still going. And I'm like, "Oh my God." One thought was, "I don't believe this, get up and go investigate." And another thought was, "Don't be a fool." [*Laughs.*] And then it stops rocking.

This is the part where a lot of people say, "Jerry, come on…" but this is no lie. The clown turned around and looked at me, but I didn't see the eyes. You've got to remember now that I'm looking at a silhouette. I'm looking at something like a shadow. It scared me. I didn't see it get out of the chair, but I know it did. I had pulled the covers over my head at that point. And then I got very close to my aunt because I wanted to scream, but I was so terrified I couldn't scream. You know what I'm saying? I was so terrified that I really couldn't scream, and I'm just holding on to my aunt. I was waiting for it to come over and throw the covers off of me or something like that, but it didn't. I was scared to death. When I woke up in the morning, I found my doll still sitting in my little red rocking chair.

My aunt finally did get rid of the rocking chair, which was cool with me, and then they sent me to North Carolina. And then I wore out a white rocking chair which was much larger and much more beautiful. [*Laughs.*]

You said your aunt summoned a demon?

Yes, she did. You know how she did it was by trying to scare me. By trying to scare me, she summoned it. Later on, little did I know that I would grow up fighting demons and I would learn their pattern. Many of the things that we think are ghosts are actually demons. I've learned that the hard way.

So you think she put the idea in your head?

We have to be very careful what we say and what we do. We're very powerful, ourselves. We are spirits. We have a spirit inside of us. I always tell people when I used to preach, one of the interesting things that God did was to let us know that we live in a world full of spirits. We're made just like Him. The scripture says, "When He shall be here, we shall see Him as He is. We shall be just like Him." Meaning that he's going to come here in spirit form. When he made man and woman, he made us in his image after his likeness. God is not flesh. He's a spirit, so when he made us, he made us the same as him. God says, "If you want to worship me, you have to worship me in spirit; that's the only way you can worship me." Well guess what, that's the way we can worship the devil too.

I've seen this happen quite a few times—we can open up a lot of things just by talking. We can open up some worlds that we don't want to open up and not even realize that we are actually opening up one of those worlds. My aunt told me I was going to see something in my rocking chair. When we open up these little things, demons say, "Great!" It's the power of suggestion. We have that power, we're very powerful.

Gino

Sterling Heights, Michigan

June 2001

Gino is 20 years old and living in the finished basement of his parents' house in Sterling Heights, Michigan. The house isn't that old; it was a new construction when he and his family moved in.

Today, life is somewhat stable for Gino, but in June of 2001, the then-16-year-old was in a tough place. He was abusing drugs, not sleeping very well, and withdrawing emotionally. From June to July of 2001, he suffered through six weeks of torment from what he describes as a demon. Before June of 2001, Gino said he had never experienced anything that he could concretely say was supernatural. He asked that his last name not be used.

What started these events back in June of 2001?

I went to bed, normal as can be. I woke up in the middle of the night—it happens to me. I look up from my bed and there is this big figure. From what I could see, he was perched on my desk like a gargoyle. Because of the way my bed is set up, my bed is parallel to my desk. When I looked up, I looked to my right, and I just see it, and then I froze.

Was there enough light in your room to see the details?

The light in my room was actually on. I saw the full-on figure. I didn't know what to make of it, really.

How long was the figure there?

It felt like forever. I don't know exactly how long. It might have been a few minutes, it might have been an hour, but it felt like forever when I was staring at it. I was shaken up, and then I passed out.

Do you think you passed out from fear?

I don't know, I wouldn't be able to tell you really.

What did you think about this the next day?

I didn't know what to think, to tell you the truth. It was one of those things I didn't know who to tell, who to talk to about it. I thought, "Eh, maybe it was just a dream." And then the second encounter happened, and that kind of reaffirmed that this isn't just a dream—this is something that's not right.

The second encounter, I don't even know if I can describe that part because it was just so freaky. I looked into the mirror and I only saw his face—I didn't see mine. I froze. But this actually seems very quick because I saw him, I froze, I blinked, and then he was gone.

Can you describe him?

He looked about 6'2" (188 cm), he had long, greasy black hair. He was unshaven, but there was, like, a permanent shadow around his eyes. He wore a long, black trench coat with a black shirt, black pants, and boots. It was a dark-complexioned Caucasian male.

At what point did you ask for help with this?

After this I decided to finally tell one of my friends. She and this other girl I know, they're big into the whole ghost thing, witchcraft, and stuff like that. I didn't know who else to tell, so I told them. So they said, "Let's have a Ouija board session." The close friend I went to, she has a ghost—she calls it her guardian angel—living inside her house. So we decided that, with a Ouija board, we're going to ask her guardian angel about this guy.

Because of the whole mirror sequence, and because I was really into the movie *Fight Club* at the time, I thought maybe this was, like, my alter ego. So I named him "Tyler." We asked her guardian angel about Tyler, and the Ouija board stopped moving. Nothing happened. We kept trying to coax her back out, but she was gone. Apparently, after I left that day she came back and started talking to my friend and telling her I should watch out because nothing good will come out of this.

My friend, a week or so after this, was going away to Australia for awhile. Before she left, being into witchcraft, she gave me a ring that, according to her and her friend—I'm still kinda leery about the whole witchcraft thing—they kind of blessed. Like a shield of protection over me. I just had to keep it on me at all times. So at that point I put it around a necklace.

So she went off to Australia, and she was gone for about two weeks. About four days into it was my third encounter. This was where I actually saw him. I stood up, and I talked to him.

What did you say?

I asked him, "Why are you here?"

When the whole encounter happened, it was kind of the same scenario where I woke up, my lights weren't on in my room, but in my basement I have a window leading out to the living room. I look out and I see the lights on in there. I look at the clock and I see that it's three or four o'clock in the morning. I'm like, "Who's still up?"

I get out of my room. I start walking, and then I see him leaning up against our foosball table. As I try to move closer, I completely freeze. I can't move anymore, but I could talk and I said, "Why are you here?" He just looked at me and said, "Just watch out for yourself." Finally my body was able to move, and I lunged at him. I went right through him and hit the floor. I must have passed out, because I woke up a couple of hours later still on the floor. I had dried blood on my lip and I was tasting blood.

At this point, I'm freaking out. I go back to my bed and I curled up into a ball with my blanket, and I started feeling an overwhelming sense of fear and anxiety—all of that stuff. I just sat there and started crying out of nowhere. Then all of these images started running through my head; just some of the most gory stuff you can possibly think about. I couldn't stop it, I'm sitting there and I must have been there for about 10 minutes before I passed out. When I woke up, I was still in that same position, curled up into a ball against my wall.

When and how did these encounters end?

My friend in Australia later told me that she was out with her friends to dinner and suddenly she just felt really weird and had to go back to the room. She entered her room again, she fell down to her knees crying, and she called me the next day and said, "What happened to you?" I told her and she was freaking out because she couldn't be here to help me with all of this.

The final encounter was by far the most tame of all of them. With this one I woke up in bed. The lights are on and as I look up, I see him standing there. I look up and I see him standing above me, like above my head area. Again I'm frozen, and he puts his

175

hand above my face and then I passed back out. I didn't know what happened at all. And then my friend called me back from Australia, apparently she fell asleep on the bus going somewhere and had a dream where her guardian angel told her that I was in trouble and they flew to my house [*"flew" as in some astral method of travel*], she came downstairs, and she saw him standing over me with his hand over my face. She started yelling at him, something like, "He's mine, you can't take him." He apparently moved away from me and pushed her up against the wall. She kept yelling stuff that he can't have me and finally he let her go and disappeared. They have this on video. I've seen the video of her sleeping on the bus and she's talking in her sleep, saying things like, "Get off him," and she was yelling at one point.

Has anything happened since?

No. Nothing.

What do you think it was, and what did it mean to you?

The best that we can explain it: He was a demon, at least according to the definition of a demon. I know at that point in my life, it was a tough time. I know that much. From what I can figure, it was where I was at my weakest, emotionally. Looking back, that would be a perfect time to strike on anybody and try and influence them. I had gotten pretty deep into a lot of things at that point… things like drugs.

Do you think this was the wake-up call to try and clean up?

I don't know. I cleaned up—of course, it's hard to clean up fully. I still haven't cleaned up fully, but my life has become a lot more stable. Even though I'm still being stupid. I'm only 20, and life's become a lot more stable than it was at that time. I believe even more now than ever that stuff like demons and ghosts, all that exists.

I kind of wish I'd see Tyler again. I don't know why; it was horrible, but it's just that…you want to know. You want to know why. You want to know how. Just so many things are left unanswered by all of this. It probably will never be answered.

Ian Yeung
Thornhill, Ontario, Canada
April 5, 2003

By some estimates, sleep paralysis—the phenomenon of waking up during your otherwise normal sleep routine to find that you recognize your surroundings, but you are literally paralyzed for a very frightening two to 10 seconds—has happened to four out of 10 people. During these episodes, some people experience more than just a frightening loss of movement—some also see visions of creatures, or even people coming toward them in this incredibly prone state. Whether the episode is visitation or spectral attack is up to the perception of the witness.

Ian Yeung is a 24-year-old graduate student studying architecture. He was born in Hong Kong, but came over to North America as a kid. On April 5, 2003, Yeung experienced a very profound event during a sleep paralysis episode. He remembers the date because he e-mailed me about it a few days afterward.

What do you remember from that night in April?

This was really different because I've had very frequent episodes, but they mostly happened when I wasn't sure if I was awake or not. But this is the only one where I believe it happened after I woke up, so I was in full consciousness.

I woke up from a dream. I can't remember the content of the dream, but the content isn't really important. I woke up and I felt myself paralyzed, and that happened to me quite often. Then suddenly I could see the corner of my room. I woke up with my head facing that way, and I saw sort of a faint profile of a person in the corner. It's hard to describe the vision; it's almost like sort of a cloud or mist forming the silhouette of a man. I could clearly see his facial expressions.

I could not move at all, I could not hear anything. In this state, it's almost like your hearing is completely cut off. That's just how it felt. There's this thing in front of me. Although it was very faint, it was weird how I could actually see his facial expressions. He looked like he was worried, or apprehensive, or something. I really don't think this was someone I've met before. He looked like an elderly Caucasian man. He was almost priest-like—maybe because he was completely white.

Whenever I had an episode, I would try very hard to shake myself out of it. To wake up. Another unique thing about this experience is that as I regained control of my body, I felt almost like vibrations of something falling down. Almost like the force, or whatever that was paralyzing me, was crumbling down. I could feel vibrations through my body as I regained control of my hands, my body, and my legs. Literally at the same time I'm gaining movement, the creature, or whatever this thing in front of me is, was fading away. I think I saw a change in the expression of his face as he was fading—it was like he was awed. As soon as I could move, I sat up and I said, "I don't know who you are. I don't care who you are. I don't have anything to do with you. Just leave and don't come back again."

This was the only time when something like this happened, and I was pretty sure that I was awake.

How often were you having these paralysis episodes?

These episodes were quite frequent for me around that time. They didn't really happen anymore after 2005 for some reason. I would say from 2000 to 2004 it happened to me very frequently. It didn't get to the point where I was disturbed, but when it happened I would think to myself, "Oh, here it goes again." I would say it happened once or twice every month back then.

During the more aggressive episodes, I could feel a presence of something, and I could almost feel something moving on my bed. Sometimes I felt cold air blowing down on me.

I've talked to some people—the more scientifically-minded ones—and they'd say, "Oh that's just sleep paralysis, blah, blah, blah…you would never die from it." I was aware that you would never die from one of these things. Chinese people actually believe that these things are common. Yeah, although you don't die from it, Chinese folklore says that these are spirits floating or existing, and they basically have to siphon your energy in order for them to exist in our world. The Chinese people believe that if you allow them to come to you, if you don't struggle your way out of these episodes, you won't die, but what they believe is that your luck, or your life, would worsen if you let them take that energy from you. So what happens is, as your luck goes down, you may get run over by a bus and stuff like that. Our people believe in that. They tend to struggle their way out whenever these things happen.

Now that you've had some years to look back on this, what do you think it was? Was it a visitation?

I think it was a spirit trying to attack, or some kind of visit. It's interesting that these episodes were happening a lot more often then, because I wasn't really happy with my life. I think that when one is more or less depressed with life, they would be more prone to these attacks. I guess that, scientifically, you can explain that when someone is depressed, they are also more prone to having hallucinations.

Would you have called yourself depressed back then?

I wouldn't say clinically depressed, but a lot of things like school, personal relationships, and things like that were not really going my way. I was admitted to a different school in September of 2004, and I'm really liking the environment. So I guess my life has improved, and as it did improve, the frequency of these episodes decreased dramatically.

When I tell this to other people, I don't necessarily say that I'm sure it was a spirit or something like that. I would say more that I wasn't in a very good state back then. I wouldn't say I was going insane or seeing things, but that I was just a lot more prone to issues.

Are you a believer in spirits now?

I have a really ambiguous stand on this issue. I cannot be sure… that's the thing. I don't want to completely eliminate the possibility that there are spirits. Besides this, I have not experienced any other thing concrete enough for me to draw the conclusion that they do exist. I know people who claim that they have seen or witnessed things, and now it's impossible for them not to believe in spirits, or ghosts because they have experienced them firsthand. But I would say, besides this episode with the old man, I have not experienced anything else concrete.

Chapter 7

Ghost Hunting

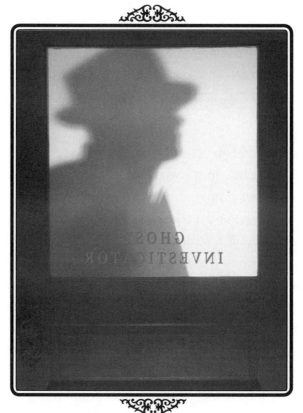

"Private Eye." Image source © istockphoto.com/Todd Smith

Ghosts are frightening because when they appear, they are often unexpected. Many people don't want to speak about the subject because of their religious belief systems or deep-seated fear of specters and spirits. But there are a growing number of people who go looking for ghosts.

Some warm summer's evening, drive through the battlefields of Gettysburg, Pennsylvania, and see how many people are out there taking photographs, holding audio recorders, or simply lurking around hoping to have a brush with the ghost of a bygone Civil War soldier. The demographic of those seeking the ghosts are diverse: old and young, men and women, even families with small children. We're intrigued with the implications of seeing a glimpse of the other side. Some people pursue the supernatural as a hobby, while for others it's their passion or maybe even their job. Ghost hunters seek spirits out, and many times they find them.

Travis Hayes
North of Albany, Louisiana
Summer of 1984

Travis Hayes is 41 years old and lives about 60 miles (97 km) north of New Orleans, in a town called Hammond, Louisiana. He makes a mean pot of gumbo and has been interested in ghosts since a young age, when he and a friend used to regularly see a man and a horse walking through a stretch of woods near the house where he grew up. Young Travis would holler hello to the strange man, but the rider never looked his way. Hayes thought the horseman was real until he realized that when the horse walked across a part of a stream that would have been a foot or two deep (30–61 cm), it didn't sink at all but went right across the top of the water. At that moment, he realized what he had been witnessing was beyond his understanding of the natural world. At that point he "ran home to momma," he says with an accent that's farther south than your traditional southern accent, but just a bit north of a bayou accent.

He currently works as a deputy in the Tangipahoa Parish Sheriff's Office, but back in 1984 he was working as a fireman. When Travis was growing up, he heard the old-timers in town talk about the legend of a gray lady and her ghostly dog who wandered a lonely logging road in a wooded part of town just north of Albany, Louisiana. Hayes never thought he'd actually see her.

What happened the day you saw her?

We were at the fire station one night, and it was 10:30 or 11 o'clock. I was getting ready to leave when one of the guys came in. His name was Luis, he was Cuban and dark-complexioned, and that night he was white as a ghost. I said, "Luis, what's wrong?"

He said "Uhhh...ahhh...." Then he just started stumbling. I said, "Calm down and tell us what happened."

He said, "I saw that witch lady."

"What witch lady?" Then he went on to describe her and tell us where the witch lady was. He said she was out near what used to be the eighth ward school. It's a church now, but it used to be an old schoolhouse. We said, "Well take us out there," and he said, "Oh no, no. I can't go." So six of us jumped into a little car, a Buick Regal, and drove out there.

We find where we figure he was talking about and pull up. This was also an area that was considered Lovers' Lane, where people would report seeing strange light shining in different colors. Luis told us you have to flash the headlights three times and wait.

I know, it sounded silly—you flash the lights three times and wait, but of course we've gotta do it. Charles was driving, Frank was in the passenger side, and Daniel was in the middle of the front seat. In the backseat was the Assistant Fire Chief, Tommy, we had Pete Junior in the middle, and me on the passenger side in the back seat.

We sat there for about an hour and nothing happened. We're all talking about this, talking about that, and we finally decided, okay, Luis is just seeing things. Nothing is going to happen. We cranked the car, we're pulling out, and all of a sudden Tommy pats me on the shoulder and he pointed out back. I look out the glass behind us, and I see a woman, gray in color, wearing a long dress, long hair, and it looks like the dress and hair were kind of blowing in the breeze. She's just standing there looking at us, and there was a dog standing beside her. They were both colored in gray. It wasn't a black dog or anything like that, and there was no red eyes or anything. But she had a dog. They both had black outlines, but the basic color was a grayish-blue. Tommy put his fingers up to his mouth and told me to be quiet, don't tell anybody. We left… but we both saw her.

We got back to the fire station, and after everybody got finished talking, saying, okay, this was a wild goose chase, you know, blah, blah, blah, Luis is crazy, he's been drinkin' or something, everybody left, and me and Tommy are still there. He said, "You ready to go back?"

I said, "Yes. Let's go."

We needed to get rid of these other idiots because somebody could get hurt out there. So now we know where to go. We go back to the same road, we go a little bit farther down the road, turn around, and we just sit and wait. After about 30 minutes, we're sitting and waiting, I'm turned sideways in my pickup truck, and I'm facing Tommy and he's facing me. Then all of a sudden we notice a light shining in the window through the windshield in front of us. We both turned and looked out the windshield, and the woman was standing about 25 yards (23 m) in front of the truck. The dog wasn't with her this time. She's in front of the truck now, it's just her, and she's just standing there. And we're like, [*whispers*] "Wow, do you see that?"

"Yeah, I see it. Is it real?"

She's kind of slumped a little bit and leaned to the right, which, sitting in my truck, would've been toward the driver's side. She made a motion and she was gone. I said, "Wow, Tommy this is great!" We were all excited. But all of a sudden Tommy's eyes get real big, his mouth falls open, he picks his finger up, and points over my shoulder. I spin around in my seat—it's a summer's night, so it's warm and the windows are down—I spin around and she's right there face-to-face with me.

All I could see was her face, and I couldn't tell you a lot about it because I started screaming like a little girl, cranked the truck, broke the key off in the ignition, and we threw gravel everywhere getting out of there. Scared me to death. She actually leaned in the window of the truck, and when I turned around she was right there almost touching noses with me. She did have eyes, they weren't empty sockets or anything like that, and she had all of the facial features and everything was a grayish blue. She almost looked like a sketch—the features were there, but there was no color to it whatsoever. She almost looked animated.

How did you hear about the "witch lady," and why flash your headlights three times?

There was a ghost light—that's what everybody called it—and there was an urban legend about how the light would change colors. Then every now and again somebody mentioned the witch lady.

What Luis and them were told was that if you parked in this area, flashed the lights three times, and waited, the witch lady would show up. From what I could find out from legends and what have you is that this woman used to live in this area in a small logging village. They say she had stolen a loaf of bread and was hung for theft and the dog was also killed. Whether the dog was hung, or just shot, or beat with a stick, I don't know, but her and the dog were both killed. This was a story I had heard most of my life growing up. I never could find any documentation to prove it, and most of the old-timers that would tell you this stuff are all pretty much dead and gone now.

Have you been back to the area since?

I've been back and there's a subdivision there now. I've talked to people, this would've been in the last two years, and nobody has seen anything. I've been talking to people over there, and a couple of people told me to leave and never come back. They don't want to hear about this kind of stuff where they live. But the people that did talk to me, they don't see anything. I've even talked to the younger folks in there that are hanging on the street. They don't see or hear anything.

John Zaffis
Stratford, Connecticut

John Zaffis has been interested in the study of the paranormal his entire life. His aunt and uncle are the renowned ghost investigators Ed and Lorraine Warren, so he was certainly exposed to the subject from a young age. Now 49 years old, he's investigated hundreds of haunting cases and has a unique perspective on ghosts, spirits, and the darker side of this field…the demonic. John is an author and lectures extensively on the subject of the paranormal. He's also appeared on many television specials covering the topic.

When did you experience your first ghost?

When I was about 15 years old, I had an apparition appear at the foot of my bed. It was very transparent and it stood there. It was very tall, and it was shaking its head back and forth. At that point in time I didn't know what to make of it. I ran downstairs and I was telling my mom about it, and she said, "Did it say anything or do anything?" And I said, "No, it just stood there and shook its head back and forth." Then she looked at me with this perplexed look and she said,

John Zaffis
Photo by Aimee Zaffis

"That was your grandfather," and I went, "What?" She said, "It's something we never really talked about, but when something was wrong or something bothered my father, he would shake his head back and forth." It's not something I would have known because I was only four years old when he died. That's when I started really getting involved with it.

I started poking around, I started going to haunted locations, and then I drove my poor uncle out of his mind until he finally let me start going on investigations with him when I was about 21, 22 years old, somewhere in that time frame. That's when I started be-boppin' around, started getting more involved with it, started talking to more people, integrating with people, and I kept saying to myself, "Okay, everybody can't be making these things up. There's something to everything." That's when I started taking it farther.

I started going on a lot of human spirit cases. Did I always believe that people got possessed? No. I'd never seen it, never experienced it. I took it a step farther and begged my uncle to death until he let me get involved with that part of it.

Can you think of a case that you worked on that has really affected you?

It's a case…let's go with just using her first name. Her name was Pat, and it was a case I was involved with for four years, and it took, I think it was 14 or 15 exorcisms to finally free her. This was in the Litchfield Hills in Connecticut.

It was a pretty horrendous type of case. There were different things that would tie in with this; it had left impressions. With I initially got involved, I was just going in like any ordinary case. As things started to develop, I realized the intensity of what was happening. Pat was a little tiny woman, and when she would go under, she would gain an enormous amount of strength. She would have knowledge of things that she shouldn't have—it was very, very intense. There were apparitions—a couple of them had appeared in her home—that really left a mark with me.

What did you see?

I had gone down into the basement because we had heard some noises down there. I thought, "Okay, cats, dogs, whatever," because the woman did have quite a few pets. So my instinct was to go down and look and see if one of the animals had gotten locked down below. I looked around and everything, and then as I turned, I saw this white formed figure near a couple of appliances—a freezer or whatever you want to call it. It started as a very transparent mass.

So naturally I stood there and I was watching to see exactly what was happening. I remember looking to the left, and looking to the right to see if there was something reflecting. There wasn't. I stood there and though it was still mostly transparent, I was able to make it out and it was actually a very beautiful woman. I was able to see some of the features; they weren't clear-cut, if you will, but that intrigued me more because I stood there and I said to myself, "They don't usually appear this way." It was one of the very few occasions like that that's happened to me.

Do you have a sense of who she might have been?

At that point in time? No. But today: Yes. I feel that it was something that just disguised itself so it would catch my interest.

So you think it was related to demonic possession?

Yes, I do. But in disguise. There were several other occasions in that house when these black figures appeared and activity kicked up instantly. As soon as I had seen them.

The final exorcism that was performed on Pat ten years ago was quite intense. It was Bishop McKenna that performed it. He was able to actually call out the last several demons that were with her, and he was able to get a couple of the names and was able to actually break the hold they had on her. Pat had ten years of peace after that. Unfortunately, she passed away in 2005, but right up until the end she said, "I'll finally be at total peace. There won't be anything lingering around me just waiting to reenter again." Because, as we know, for people that go through this, demons always have that window where they just wait for the right opportunity to reenter again.

Was that your first confrontation with what you refer to as a demon?

No. There were several cases where they were really monumental. Where you say, okay, we're dealing with the real thing here, and this person is definitely a possessed type of individual. Those are few and far between. People being oppressed? Yes. But possession, it's rare, and when you do come up against that, you know it.

How do you know? What are some of the signs?

Some of the particular type things that end up happening is people have this knowledge about things. They gain an enormous amount of strength. You feel your energy get strained from you when you're working on these types of cases. I've experienced that several times in cases.

What happens?

You get extremely discombobulated, you get very, very tired—and it's not a normal type of tired, you get totally drained. You know the difference after you've experienced it several different times. You do realize what to look for and what to watch for.

How has doing this work affected you?

What happens is the more you get involved, and the more you delve in, especially on the demonology end of it, you have to keep reevaluating and you have to keep looking at the different perspectives that occur and how they intertwine. The different religions, their different purposes. Now, are all exorcisms successful? No. Sometimes they do have to be repeated. I mean, do I just jump in and say somebody is possessed? No. I'm interested in, hey, have you been to any doctors? Is there anything physically wrong with you? Are you on medications? That's the way I go about it.

What's going through your mind when you see these things after doing it for so long? Are the phenomena not as profound as they once were?

They always are. To me, they always are. To this day, 33 years later, I still stand there in a state of awe. You know this is happening, I realize it's happening, and one of the worst things with me is I get so tied up into the moment, you know, are the cameras rolling? [*Laughs.*] Are we documenting this? And a lot of times unfortunately when these things occur, you never have your equipment set up or you never even have it with you.

Were you raised in a particular religion?

I was raised Roman Catholic.

Thinking back to when you saw your first ghost at age 15, were you buying in to Catholicism at that point?

No. Back in the 70s we questioned everything. There wasn't anything you didn't question. I grew up hearing about ghosts, I always heard all of the stories. I didn't believe it because I never witnessed anything. But when I looked at it, I said to myself, "There has to be something to all this."

At what point in doing this work do your experiences cement your faith in Roman Catholicism?

It was a combination of a lot of things occurring. Watching some of the different things that occurred with people, watching what people had gone through. There's so much that I have seen that really made me start to think of what I believed in. I was brought up and raised Roman Catholic, but big deal. That wasn't a factor to me early on. But the more I got involved, the more different types of clergy, the different religions, and seeing some of the different things that occurred, it made me sit back and evaluate. I still do that. I still sit back and I evaluate.

When you start talking about the demonology end of it, I always try to incorporate so much of what I do into it. This subject is much more acceptable now than it ever was before. It's just a strange, strange world.

What keeps you doing this work after so many years?

Knowledge. Knowledge. The quest of understanding it. My favorite term is the paranormal because it's the unknown. It's still that drive. I want to meet that old monk; I want to pick his brain. What's he been through? I want to meet the old Indian chief. What's he been through? The different cultures, the different belief systems, that drive is still very much there. It's still my quest.

Do I ever think I'm going to have the answers? No. I don't think any of us will ever have those answers that so many are seeking, but it's great to be able to unravel a few things, and put a few things into perspective.

Bill Jimenez, Ph.D.
San Diego, California 1962
and Pico Rivera, California 2004-2005

Bill Jimenez has been interested in ghosts since he saw his first when he was 12 years old. Bill has been a paranormal investigator for more than half of his life, and his background makes him rather uniquely qualified to look into this type of phenomenon. He's been a police officer for more than 30 years and is currently a state of California law enforcement officer, and he also has a doctorate in psychology.

The 55-year-old currently has a paranormal investigation team whose members include other police officers, attorneys, a historian, a writer, and a psychic. Bill isn't out to make a name for himself or his group; they don't even have a Web site. Studying this subject and helping people (both the living and the dead) is simply his passion.

How did you get interested in the subject?

I was 12 years old and we lived in this old house in San Diego. I'm pretty sure the people who owned the house before were making illegal alcohol, you know, bootleggers. My brother and I, we used to go down to the basement and there were these huge barrels and some equipment, which now I know was distilling equipment. So anyway, what I couldn't understand was that in some places in the house were these cold spots. The interesting thing was that when I first moved into the house, I saw this old guy walking down the hallway. I was 12 years old, so what did I know? But then this specific area of the house was very cold all of the time. I didn't want to make a big deal about it, but it turns out, and I found this out maybe 25 years later, that this old guy was haunting my mom.

And that's what you saw?

Yeah, the old guy. I found out this old guy was haunting my mom, and he really wanted to communicate with her. My parents, I guess they didn't want us to get scared so they tried not to talk about it, but I used to see the old guy. Then afterwards I got scared because I would see him go through the walls. That's when I told my mom, you know, I'm seeing this guy, and she said, "That's the same guy that I see, but he wants to talk to me." Other than that, she just didn't want to talk about the subject.

It so happens that my room was located right where you go down to the basement. Every night I was scared, I'd get, like, 50 blankets and throw them over me. I was scared. But that was my first encounter with the paranormal.

I became a police officer down the line in 1974. I was 24 years old. Then I was a detective, and there was a report of animal sacrifices at Will Rogers State Park. They reported blood, and hearts of cats, and everything—they had animal sacrifices that were part of a satanic ritual. I didn't know much about it, so I met this deputy sheriff who was with the L.A. County Sheriffs. He was a psychologist and his forte was paranormal psychology—he knew about the science and the meaning of everything, so I was very impressed with the guy. I said, wow, I want to know more about it, so I started studying everything I could get my hands on, you know books and things. And after that, I went to college and I got a doctorate in psychology.

The word got out that I like to study ghosts, so people started calling me to go to their houses to see what I can find out. I started doing that 31 years ago, I've been a cop for 32 years. I've been investigating ghosts as much as bad guys.

I started doing a lot of investigations, and after that I started recruiting other police officers. First of all, they thought I was nuts. I'd say, "Hey, man, I went to this house…." Especially this house in Maywood where they claimed that they saw shadows at night, and even in the daytime. They'd hear knocking noises and the entities would hide things from them.

My mom, she knew that I was heavily into ghosts because of the experiences we had in San Diego, so she began to refer clients to me. I say "clients," I didn't charge, but you know, she referred people to me. So I went to the Maywood house, and sure enough something was there. You know, I'm not a psychic, I don't claim to be psychic or anything, but you develop a sixth sense when you do something for so many years.

I would imagine being a police officer has something to do with that.

You get trained to look for what's not there. I'm also a detective, and I was also in what's called criminal intelligence. I did investigations on any arrests when it came to elected officials—I did judges, those kinds of investigations. We get a lot of training about facial expressions—you can tell when people are lying, so you develop a good knack for finding the truth.

So anyway, I go to this house and I speak to the people to make sure that they don't need a psychiatrist instead of a parapsychology investigator. You want to see if they're legit. You know, a lot of people can have some problems—exterior problems that don't have anything to do with ghosts or entities. So I do that first.

When that family came to me 25 years ago, I spoke to the whole family to see that they were okay, and they were. So what we had here was an entity that would appear...usually entities will choose one person in the house or two, not all of the persons see them. So the victim—I call her "victim" because she was the one who was chosen—she was a young girl, about 12, 13, and when you have a young girl you say, okay, poltergeist: that could be causing this. So you have to do an investigation on the girl to make sure she doesn't have any traumas, you have to debunk yourself before you start. But everything was okay with the girl—she didn't have any problems, she was a good student—so that was good. So then she told me what she saw, and what she saw was her brother.

Her brother had died of AIDS about a year earlier, so she was seeing her brother. Her brother would come to her because he felt guilty that he had died of AIDS, and the family kind of disowned him because these were Hispanics—back 25 years ago, you didn't want to deal with that. But along with the brother came another entity, too, and that one she did not recognize. She was not afraid of the brother, but she was afraid of this other entity.

So I went in and I spent the night. I went by myself, I spent the night and, yeah, sure enough, I stayed in the room with the young girl in a chair. And all of a sudden the room started getting cold, and then I saw the shadow, and then I didn't see anymore. But the young lady was talking to someone. I felt the presence, I initially saw the shadow, and then it's funny, from the corner of my eye, I saw another shadow—it was the other entity that was coming in. I said, okay there was something there.

I still have a lot of friends that are psychics, so when I want to be sure of something, I go to them and I say, "Can you come to this house?" I don't tell them anything as to the occurrences. I'd say, "I'm doing some work in this house. Can you come with me?" So this lady named Anita, she was from Honduras, she was very good, she came with me, and sure enough she said, "Yes, there are two spirits here. One is 20 and the other is 80." Just like this. And then she described them just like the victim had described them.

She said, "I will spend the night Saturday night." So she and I and the whole family were there. The family was in the living room and somehow this room was the vortex—the most active part of the house. The psychic spoke to the [*spirit of the*] young man, and he said he wanted to apologize to his dad for being how he was. So we brought the dad in the room and I said, "You have to make peace with your son. If you don't forgive him, he's not going to go to rest. He's waiting for forgiveness. Can you tell him you forgive him and it's okay, and tell him to go to the light?"

If they're Catholic, you talk about God. If they're not Catholic, you don't talk about God. So I told him, "Tell him to go with God." I said, "Maybe you cannot hear him back, but just tell him what you feel." So the dad spoke to the son, and he was able to move on.

Now the other entity it turns out was the original owner of the house. In fact, he built the house and he didn't want to go. When the psychic spoke to him, he said, "Well, this is my house. I don't want to go." So we had to do some serious talking to the guy. Through the psychic, I said, "You know you're dead. You died I don't know how many years ago. You died and are no longer a living person, you're a spirit." So we had to convince him that he's dead. Sometimes they know they're dead, and they want to hang around, and sometimes they don't.

A week later I checked back with them, and the house was quiet.

You can tell when there's something in the house because ghosts are composed of electromagnetic energy, so you can feel it. You can feel the energy in the house and also when you go to do an investigation, you look for the lights going off and on, and the smells. That was my major investigation, and after that I started recruiting professional people. In my present team right now, we have prosecuting attorneys and police officers, and we also have psychics on our investigation team. We don't make a big what-to-do about our team. We don't have a Web site or anything because we're kind of quiet about our activities.

What is one of your most profound cases?

The case we had in Pico Rivera. This entity, they saw him as a shadow in the house. A young lady saw him and the mom saw him, so we had two people who saw this. That house is hot, I'll tell you. Extremely hot. We have gone there two years doing an ongoing investigation. We've helped entities cross over, and then more entities come over—in fact, I was there two weeks ago. They're getting better, but what we have here is a hot spot, meaning that something happened there many, many, many years ago. It's something that's there.

What we have in this family is a mom, a daughter, and the son—they're highly psychic. The theory is that when you're psychic, you're on the same frequency as the entities so they come to you. It doesn't matter where you go, they come to you. And that's why you're able to see things that other people don't see. And you can hear things. We have people here that are highly advanced. The young lady, she's 25, but she has the mind of an eight year old because she's mentally retarded. So unknowingly, she invites entities.

You see, if there's any kind of dormant entities there minding their own business, in their own dimension, she calls them. That's what we have in this house. They're being invited, someone calls them.

Now this entity named Samuel, he was constantly appearing to this young lady, and then the mom saw him. They were scared and so they called me. I briefed my team and we called Amy. She's a young psychic, and she's come a long way. She's 22 years old, and she makes some of those famous psychics look like beginners. [*Laughs.*] She has gotten so good. So we don't tell Amy anything. We bring her over and she usually works with me. She goes, "Bill, he doesn't want us in here. He says to go away." I said, "No, tell him we're not going away. Tell him we're here to help him."

Amy is the kind of person that, in order to communicate, she does not have to allow anyone to go in her body. She can see them and she can talk to them without any transformation, going into trance, or anything—she's that's good. We hadn't told Amy anything about what happened, and as soon as we got there she knew who the guy was and she spoke to him.

Bill Jimenez with psychic Amy Mayernick at the Pico Rivera house. Photo by Tamara Thorne.

To make a long story short, his name was Samuel and he was half Indian and half Spanish. This specific location in Pico Rivera was a Gabrielino Indian village that flooded many, many years ago. You also have the Spaniards, who came in the 1700s. So this guy was of mixed heritage. He was constantly being beaten by Spaniards and Indians because 100 years, 150 years ago, if you were a half anything, nobody wanted you. So he suffered a lot of pain.

Once we make contact with him, I was speaking to him. He could listen to me, but I could not hear him. But Amy was telling me what he was saying. He thought he was still alive, so we had to convince him that he had died. You can't just say, "Hey, you're dead."

You have to break it slowly. We gave therapy to this entity for three hours. I had to convince him that he died.

He said he was beaten up by men by the river—which would've been the Spaniards who came to attack him—and he said, "I was hiding." I had to convince him that I could show him a place to go where he doesn't have to hide.

He was always in pain, he said, "My neck hurts, my lower back hurts." What happened was, he was beaten and hung. I said, "Samuel, you're dead." And there was a long pause…. I told him there's a place you can go. There's a tunnel, there's a light, and you go over to the other side and you're going to be happy.

I didn't use any religious references because you don't want to go there if you don't know their beliefs—he might be insulted.

You're talking about the spirit, Samuel's beliefs here?

Right, about the spirit. So I was giving therapy to a dead person. I convinced him to go. That's where the psychology part comes in because you, in essence, are counseling entities.

For the people we have helped, they feel secure, because for example, this house in Pico Rivera, tons of people wanted to come to her house. She thought they were kind of weird, they were kooky, she didn't feel comfortable. But when she spoke to me, she felt comfortable. I don't have a Web site, I don't claim to be anything. I do it because it's a hobby for me and my guys. Our profession kind of gives us more leeway for people to trust us. Because it can be kind of weird, if you're going to leave a bunch of people in your house overnight, when you come back the next morning, the TV might be gone. [*Laughs.*] Being a professional, people trust us. They say, "These guys are cops."

We don't try to convince anybody about the existence of ghosts. We try to stay on the scientific side. For example, at the Pico Rivera house, we actually got shadows coming from the wall, a wall that the lady of the house reported kind of vibrates. So what we did was we tried to recreate the shadows. Every time we get something we try to debunk ourselves, make sure nothing else caused it, because we're the big skeptics.

Chapter 8

Ghosts Out and About

"Foggy Day 1." Photo source: © istockphoto.com/Roger Pilkington

Buildings and houses aren't the only places that can be haunted. Boats, forests, and even busy town streets all have their share of ghostly legends. It would seem ghosts can appear at any time and in any place.

Erika Emal
Aix en Provence, France
June 1996

Many ghost encounters happen in fleeting moments—within a few seconds the episode is over, but the effects are felt for many years after. In June of 1996, Erika Emal, her mother, and a friend were visiting Aix en Provence and were enjoying a night on the town when a strange young girl approached and spent the next few hours with them.

Erika is a 33-year-old painter who went to art school at L'Ecole Marchutz in Aix, so she knew her way around the ancient and historical town. But she had no idea who this peculiar visitor who took a liking to her and her mother was.

What brought you back to Aix in June of 1996?

We went for la Fête de la Musique—the music festival. It's very big in Aix. It was my mom's first time there. My mom really loves old places, and this place was just up her alley because it was founded in the first or second century B.C. They still have Roman ruins there.

I knew all of the bars to go to and all the good places to hang out. My mom and I and a friend of mine from New Zealand went to a bar. We eventually left this bar because they were closing and it was late. While we were walking out, we heard this music in the empty streets. We're walking down this cobblestone road, trying to find where this music is coming from, and we find this little party going on in the square just two squares up from where we were. We couldn't pass it up because it was music like the Gypsy Kings, and we love the Gypsy Kings—they're actually from that area and it was their nephews who were playing all their music. There were about ten people out in the square, one of the bars was open, and the guys are out there just playing their little instruments.

Out of nowhere appears this waif, as my mom called her. I mean, she must've been 17 or 18. She was this very strange girl with dark, wavy hair that looked like she routinely cut it herself. It was a mess. And she was wet, which we didn't understand unless she had jumped in a fountain somewhere. She was wearing what looked like an undergarment—like an underdress made of some kind of gauze or cheesecloth type-thing. It was all knotted up and ratty. The homeless people, if there are any in that region, don't even dress like that. I have a passion for collecting old clothes as well, and I actually bought some from an antique shop over there. What this girl was wearing looked like it was 14th, 15th century.

The girl spoke an odd dialect of French. But when she spoke to my mom, she actually spoke English to her a little bit, too. My mom said that she kept touching her face and telling her, "You're good, you're good," while holding her face on both sides—she said this in English. This girl was so connected to my mom. She literally came out of nowhere. She's just dancing, and dancing, and dancing, and no one else seemed to have even noticed her. My mom and I thought maybe they were used to her or something because she was just nutty. We couldn't believe it.

Out of nowhere, she'd start screaming, and nobody seemed to notice but us. Just literally screaming like a screechy scream. And that's while all the music is playing.

My mom went to buy this girl a glass of wine at one point, and when she handed it to her, the girl didn't grab it and it fell straight to the ground, and the girl started crying. Why she didn't take it is kind of strange, too. [*Laughs.*] You know, free glass of wine in France…. The girl kept grabbing my mom's face and touching her hair. My mom said her hands were just like ice.

The night's going on and it's getting late—it was probably at least four in the morning—and we decided that we were going to head on to the hotel. When we started to leave, the girl just started crying and sobbing and grabbing onto my mom.

She was following us, and then she stopped off to go to the bathroom. My friend and I were standing on one edge of the corner, and my mom and the girl were on the other edge. My friend and I couldn't see the girl, but we could see my mom. My mom was standing right on the edge, just a head's turn away from me and from this girl—no more than 3 feet (1 m) from her.

My mom turned to look at the girl and she was completely gone. And she had previously been in the street. She just totally disappeared. No noise. Nothing. Just nothing.

This was in the center of town, and the streets are the old, original cobblestones.

Was there any place where the girl could have ducked in to?

Number one, my mom would've heard her if she moved. From where we were to where the next little niche where someone could hide was probably a city block at least—and that's just where there was a niche. The next street didn't come for a distance of probably two blocks. There wasn't a little facade or anything in that building. But we would've seen her running either way. It was just so creepy.

So we looked for 15 minutes for this girl. I don't know why we were so concerned, but I guess maybe we thought she was homeless, or lost, or maybe she got nabbed by somebody. But of course my mom would've noticed that.

So we kept looking and looking, and we kept hearing the same screechy howl that she made earlier. It was another two blocks up from this building where we first stopped. It's like an old housing building, I would think probably from around the 1400s or 1500s because that area was from around the time. We kept being drawn back to that place—it seemed like that's where this howling was coming from. As soon as we would turn around and go some of the way toward the building, the noise would get louder. So that just spooked us.

We started going back to the hotel, which was another two blocks down the street, and as we approached the hotel, the screeching stayed at the same volume. It was like we were right there next to it, or whatever it was was following us. It was very weird. As soon as we stepped foot into the hotel, it stopped. We actually went back there the next day and took pictures in front of that building to see if we would catch anything.

Did you know of any legends in that area about any ghost girls or anything like that?

There are a million legends there. That town is so old; it's one of the first Roman provinces. The cholera epidemic wiped out most of that town at one point. My mom was thinking maybe this was one of them, one of the people killed by the disease. And I was thinking why would she be wet? Maybe she drowned somewhere over there.

Are you convinced this girl was a spirit?

The way she appeared, the way she disappeared, the way she acted, and the way no one noticed that she was there was just all too strange. It was beyond strange. My mom and I are pretty convinced. My friend from New Zealand, he doesn't have an opinion either way. He just said, "That was very strange, and I don't know what it was." Today my mom calls the girl her "little spirit friend."

When the girl was dancing around looking all nutty, we just thought she was drunk. The strangest thing for us was that we thought everybody should have been watching this girl. The way she was behaving, the way she would scream or cry and then stop, and smile, and dance around. We just thought that everybody should have been looking at her, but they didn't seem to notice that she was even there. It didn't really occur to us at the time that she might not be of this world. When she disappeared, we were like, "Did anybody else see that?"

Lokela Dakine
La'ie, Oahu, Hawaii
July 1990

Lokela Dakine is a 29-year-old, self-employed computer programmer who has lived just south of Salt Lake City, Utah, since 2000, but he did most of his growing up on the Oahu island of Hawaii. Lokela is the name he took while in Hawaii, an approximate translation of his real first name. He prefers to use his Hawaiian name because he identifies so much with that culture and because he prefers to remain anonymous to members of his Mormon faith who may frown on the discussion of ghosts.

Hawaii is a land full of legends, superstitions, and the supernatural. Dakine learned about many local legends when he first moved to the village of La'ie on Oahu. He never realized that one day he might actually come face to face with one such legend.

When did your family move to Hawaii?

It was 1985 when my family moved to Hawaii. It takes awhile for an outsider, a *haole*, to really get integrated into the culture.

What is a haole?

It's a white person, or an outsider. When Hawaiians make a friend, it lasts forever. There's so many people that come to the islands; they stay there for one semester or one year partying, and then they leave. So the Hawaiians don't open up and invite you in until after you pass a certain trial period. I was young. I was in, like, 4th grade when we moved over there, and I moved into a village that mostly had other people that were there due to work. So there was lots of turnover in that village. But because of that I was able to get into the culture faster than most others.

How long does it take to get integrated into the culture there?

Years...a year or two before you get any real friends. Before that they'll hang out, but they don't talk that much. I went through elementary school there, and in fourth grade I learned all of the Hawaiian superstitions, and legends, and culture, and stuff like that. I had friends that were interested in the paranormal, and we had the usual local urban legends about this plantation house or that plantation house being haunted, and we'd go with our flashlights at night. And of course we didn't find anything in those plantation houses. We just scared ourselves silly. [*Laughs.*]

I was involved with the Boy Scouts, so we went on all of these scout trips as well, and we talked about the Pukukea lady and other legends. She's a lady that supposedly haunts one of the Boy Scout camps on the north shore of Oahu. So anyway, I got versed in the Hawaiian superstition stuff. They even told us that ti leaves are supposed to keep away the evil spirits—everyone has these ti leaves growing in their yards to protect themselves from unwanted spirits.

In 1990, I guess I would have been 14. I was at another Boy Scout camp, and over there it's a little different than here on the mainland. It doesn't get cold at night. They think it does, but it doesn't. [*Laughs.*] So we don't use real tents; we just put up a couple of poles and tie a tarp to it, just to protect us from the wind and rain a little.

At this camp we went to Hukilau Beach, and that's just a good place to camp and body surf—not really good waves for regular surfing, but it's a good spot. At the end of Hukilau Beach, there's the Hukilau River. Hukilau River marks the end of my village; that's where La'ie ends and Kahuku begins.

(To understand the significance of La'ie, Dakine went into some Hawaiian history.)

Hawaii was settled a long, long time ago. They had a feudal system of government. Each island was ruled by a king. This king was normally called an Ali'i Nui, and each island was subdivided into villages ruled by a chief, an Ali'i. There was also one city of refuge on each island, and basically the city of refuge is a place where the king's soldiers cannot go. If you make it to the city of refuge before the king's men get you, you're safe.

Hawaii used to have some very strict laws. Women weren't even allowed to eat bananas; they could get clubbed to death for eating a banana, or stepping on the sandal of someone who outranks you. There were tons of strict laws, and most of them ended up with you getting beaten to death. [*Laughs.*] So if you break any small law, you run to the city of refuge. The king knows about the rule, he knows you can enter the city of refuge. Because of boundary disputes, they put up three temples marking where the city of refuge begins and ends. These temples are called heiau. The city of refuge on Oahu is where the current village or town of La'ie is located. And that's where I grew up.

So La'ie was the city of refuge?

That was the city of refuge. So we've got a whole bunch of neat stuff in La'ie. Anyways, the king would send his men, his soldiers, the night marchers, or the ka huaka'i Po, to circle around the city of refuge every so often to try and catch anyone sneaking in or out. The criminals, they figure that after a while the king is going to forget, so they can sneak back out of the city of refuge. But if they get caught by the night marchers, they still get in trouble.

Local legend has it that these soldiers, these night marchers, they still walk on their trails. They still do it—even though thousands of years have passed, their spirits still walk the trails.

Is there any danger in seeing the night marchers, according to the legends?

According to the legends, if you see them, you've got to know how to act. If you don't, you get beaten to death. [*Laughs.*] If you don't react the right way, they think that you're one of the criminals trying to sneak in or sneak out. I've got a cousin living on the big island, and on the big island they say you're supposed to prostrate yourself—you know, bow down before them, don't look at them, and then they'll pass. By bowing down, you show that you recognize them.

So the night marchers are on more than one island?

Yeah, there's the city of refuge on every island, and La'ie is just one of the trails on Oahu.

So in 1990, my scout troop was camped right there on the beach, where the beach meets up with the river, which is right at the edge of the city of refuge. It's kind of an interesting spot because everyone believes in ghost stories, sort of, but they laugh at them at the same time. And we were all 14-year-old boys, so we wanted to prove how brave we were. As is common at scout camps, we joked and we talked until the wee hours of the morning. We went to bed around 1:30 or 2 o'clock in the morning, somewhere in there. But on that night, shortly after we went to bed, we heard some flutes and some drums in the air. It was already dark, so we really couldn't see much.

Were there any houses or anything nearby?

We were off toward the river side, which people don't live by. So we hear the flutes, we hear some drums, I'm in a tent with a friend, we look up, and there's this fog that's going along the border of the river, going from the mountain down toward the beach. As this fog gets closer to us—and it's just a column, it's not like universal fog like you see on the east coast of the mainland—it's a column, you know? And as it gets closer, the sound of the drums and the flutes get louder, and we start hearing some marching feet. We had no idea what to do. We think that it might be the night marchers, but our minds were still a little skeptical. I mean, those are ghost stories that everyone tells, but no one really believes. So we decide that we'd play along, and we go back into our sleeping bags and hide our faces.

Were you really scared at this point, or were you just playing along?

A little of both.

Did you think someone was playing a prank?

Yeah. We were also known for our pranks. So I was a bit scared, but not enough to admit it to anyone. So we hide there with our faces hidden in our sleeping bags until the sound subsides. After a while the mist had gone, and we did get a little sleep. And when the sun rose the next morning, we awoke and found hundreds, if not thousands, of footprints—you know, man-sized footprints, like 11 inches (28 cm) long—going from the river along the beach. No one had any explanation.

Did any of the other kids or the scout leaders claim to hear anything the next morning?

Not really. They were talking in small groups. I was talking with my three closest friends in the scout troop—they all admitted to hearing something, but no one would describe what that something was. It was a church scout troop, so you've got a whole bunch of 14-year-old Christian boys with their scout leaders contemplating, "What if this one aspect of the Hawaiian religion was true?"

Glossary

afterlife A realm in which many believe an individual's consciousness will continue to reside after death.

ambiguous Vague, open to more than one interpretation.

atrocity Something that is extremely wicked, horrifying, violent, or barbaric.

charismatic Defined by a power of leadership, charm, and appeal.

controversy A dispute or misunderstanding of opposing views.

crematory A furnace used to reduce a dead body to ashes.

depression A state of feeling sad, often due to a psychological disorder.

detrimental Harmful or damaging.

euphoria A feeling of well-being or happiness.

eyewitness One who sees an event, often a crime, as it is taking place.

hostile Unfriendly.

medium An individual held to be a communicator between the living and the dead.

paralyzed Defined by a complete or partial loss of function or feeling in the body.

paranormal Lacking the ability to be defined by science.

phenomenon An event that cannot be explained by science.

picturesque Charming, resembling a painted scene or picture.

priory A religious house, run by a prior.

prohibition The act of making illegal the manufacture, transportation, and sale of alcoholic beverages.

psychic A person who claims to have the ability to see and sense information or events, like spirits, hidden from the normal senses.

skeptical Having a questioning attitude toward facts, opinions, or beliefs.

slaughterhouse A facility where animals are killed and processed for food consumption.

supernatural Above the laws of nature, or existing outside of the physical world.

transient An individual who does not stay in one place for a long time, choosing to relocate frequently.

translucent Allowing light, but not detailed images, to pass through.

transparent Allowing light and clear images to pass through.

For More Information

American Association of Paranormal Investigators
13973 East Utah Circle
Aurora, CO 80012
(720) 339-4381
Web site: http://www.ghostpi.com/Main.htm
An association dedicated to paranormal research and investigation.

The American Ghost Society
15 Forest Knolls Estates
Decatur, IL 62521
(217) 422-1002
Web site: http://www.prairieghosts.com/ags.html
An organization that seeks to find and authenticate evidence of ghosts
   and the paranormal.

Association TransCommunication
P.O. Box 13111
Reno, NV 89507
Web site: http://atransc.org
An organization dedicated to learning more about the communication
   between the living and the dead.

The Ghost Investigators Society
P.O. Box 2383
Layton, UT 84041
Web site: http://www.ghostpix.com/index.htm
A group of investigators who seek out ghostly phenomena and correct
   misconceptions about them to the public.

Metropolitan Museum of Art
1000 Fifth Avenue
New York, NY 10028-0198
(212) 535-7710
Web site: http://www.metmuseum.org
One of the world's largest and finest art museums with collections that
    include more than two million works of art spanning five thousand
    years of world culture, from prehistory to the present and from
    every part of the globe.

Web Sites

Due to the changing nature of Internet links, Rosen Publishing has
developed an online list of Web sites related to the subject of this book.
This site is updated regularly. Please use this link to access the list:

http://www.rosenlinks.com/HAUNT/Ghost

For Further Reading

Anson, Jay. *The Amityville Horror.* New York, NY: Pocket Star, 2005.

Bailey, Diane. *Ghosts in America.* New York, NY: Rosen Publishing, 2011.

Belanger, Jeff. *Ghosts of War: Restless Spirits of Soldiers, Spies, and Saboteurs.* New York, NY: Rosen Publishing, 2009.

Belanger, Jeff. *Paranormal Encounters: A Look at the Evidence.* New York, NY: Rosen Publishing, 2011.

Belanger, Jeff. *World's Most Haunted Places.* New York, NY: Rosen Publishing, 2009.

Belanger, Michelle. *The Ghost Hunter's Survival Guide: Protection Techniques for Encounters with the Paranormal.* Woodbury, MN: Llewellyn, 2009.

Bodine, Echo. *The Little Book of True Ghost Stories.* Newburyport, MA: Hampton Roads, 2011.

Bodine, Michael. *Growing Up Psychic: From Skeptic to Believer.* Woodbury, MN: Llewellyn, 2010.

Brown, Beth. *Conducting a Paranormal Investigation: A Training Guide.* Richmond, VA: Iron Cauldron Books, 2008.

Ellis, Melissa Martin. *The Everything Ghost Hunting Book: Tips, Tools, and Techniques for Exploring the Supernatural World.* Avon, MA: Adams Media, 2009.

Haughton, Brian. *Famous Ghost Stories: Legends and Lore.* New York, NY: Rosen Publishing, 2011.

James, M. R. *Collected Ghost Stories.* New York, NY: Oxford, 2011.

Jones, Marie D. *Modern Science and the Paranormal.* New York, NY: Rosen Publishing, 2009.

Lew, Kristi. *Monsters, Beasts, and Demons in America.* New York, NY: Rosen Publishing, 2011.

Lynch, Gordon J., Diane Canwell, and Jonathan Sutherland. *Famous Ghosts and Haunted Places.* New York, NY: Rosen Publishing, 2011.

Mills, J. Elizabeth. *Witches in America.* New York, NY: Rosen Publishing, 2011.

Norman, Michael and Beth Scott. *Haunted America.* New York, NY: Tor Books, 2007.

Pye, Michael and Kirsten Dalley. *Ghosts, Specters, and Haunted Places.* New York, NY: Rosen Publishing, 2012.

Wilder, Annie. *Trucker Ghost Stories: And Other True Tales of Haunted Highways, Weird Encounters, and Legends of the Road.* New York, NY: Tor Books, 2012.

Zepke, Terrance. *A Ghost Hunter's Guide to the Most Haunted Places in America.* Sebastopol, CA: Safari Publishing, 2012.

Index

A

AIDS, 196
Aix en Provence, France, 204
Albany, Louisiana, 182
Albuquerque, New Mexico, 152
Alice Through the Looking Glass, 150
Amityville, New York, 14-15
Anchorage, Alaska, 44
Angel of Death, 56-59
Anglican priest, 29, 76
Anson, Jay, 29
Archer Avenue, 9
Astrodome, 39
Austin, Texas, 123

B

baseball player, major-league, 39
Benson, Vermont, 105
Bible, the, 11, 92, 155
Birmingham, England, 50
Bishop McKenna, 189
Blessed Virgin, 80
bootleggers, 193
Boston, Massachusetts, 95
Boy Scouts, 210
Breadsall Priory, 148
Brolin, James, 17
Brooklyn, New York, 168
Brooksville, Florida, 82

C

Cardinals, St. Louis, 39
cat ghost, 108
Chicago, Illinois, 9, 152
Chinese folklore, 179
Christian Scientist, 78
city of refuge, 211
Civil War,
    connection to, 142
    reenactors, 142
    toys, 38
cleft palate, born with a, 43
Clifton Forge, Virginia, 160
cobblestone road, 204
cold spot, 20, 50
Crocker Hall, 33

D

Dayton, Tennessee, 118
DeFeo murders, 15
Depression, the Great, 40
Derby, England, 148
Desert Sands Inn, 153
Dix, Linda, 36
doppelganger, 48
Duke University, 29

E

East Bridgewater, Massachusetts, 33
Eisenhower Room, the, 146
exorcism, 29, 188

F

Farnsworth House, the, 142
feet, pinching of, 51
Fête de la Musique, la 204
Fight Club, 174
fireproof glass, 19
Firestone mansion, 89
floating above the room, 162
footsteps,
    in the rug, 71
    hearing, 37, 147
Foyil, Oklahoma, 88
Framingham, Massachusetts, 33
Framingham State College, 33

G

Gabrielino Indian village, 199
Garret Room, the, 143
Gettysburg, 9, 38, 142
Gino, 172
Grove, Oklahoma, 39
Gypsy Kinds, 205

H

Hammond, Louisiana, 182
haole, 209
harlequin pattern, 24
Hawaiian superstition, 210
Hog Island, Rhode Island, 94
hooded figure, 58
Horton Grand Hotel, 131
Hukilau Beach, 210

Huron, South Dakota, 92-93
hurricanes, 82

I
imprint of a hand, 35
Indianapolis, Indiana, 101
Indians, local, 65

J
Jasper, Tennessee, 108
Jesuit mission, 65
Jewish tradition, 155
Jimenez, Bill, 192
Johanna, 135

K
Kahuku, 210
Kingsbury, Rev. Father Scott E., 76

L
Las Vegas strip, 133
L'Ecole Marchutz, 204
Lehman, Suzy, 108
Le'Kay, Janie, 50
Lent, 24
life after death, proof of, 10
lightning, 76
Lindenhurst, Illinois, 56
Lindenhurst, New York, 16
Litchfield Hills, Connecticut, 188
Long Island, 20
Los Angeles, California, 76
Lutz, George, 14
Lyman Hall, 128

M
Mackey, Bobby, 135
Mather, Michael K., 131
McKenna, Bishop, 189
Methodist, 18
Mets, New York, 39
middle way, the, 80
Mormon faith, 209

N
Nashville, 138
natural phenomena, 76
near-death experiences, 159-160
Neighbor, Jennifer, 126
New Orleans, 24
New Palestine, Indiana, 101
New Zealand, 204
night marchers, the, 212
nonorthodox priest, 76
North Carolina, 168
nursing facility, 122

O
Oahu, Hawaii, 210, 221
oral tradition, 9
Oregon, 152
owl in the closet, 49
Ozarks, the, 152

P
Palace Station Hotel, 133
paralysis, sleep, 177
pattern of protection, 24
Peirce Hall, 33

pennies, dropping 104
Phoenix, Arizona, 152
photography, spirit, 112
Pico Rivera, California, 192
pinches, 51, 146
possessions, 188
power of suggestion, the, 172
Prentice Hall, 29
Pukukea Lady, 210
Purgatory, 80

Q
quantum physics, 61

R
red room, 22
resonance changes, 20
River Street Inn, 126
Rockville Center, 18
Rockwood, Michigan, 98
Roman Catholic,
    church, 191
    priest, 29

S
Salem, Virginia, 112
Samuel, entity named, 198
San Diego, California, 32, 131, 192
Savannah, Georgia, 126
Schultz Room, the, 143
Scream movies, 98
sensationalism, 11
sleep paralysis, 177

sleeping, 168
South Dakota, 133
spirit,
    children, 147
    photography, 112
spooks, 61
Springfield, Missouri, 88
St. Mary of the Angels, 79
Sterling Heights, Michigan, 172
Stratford, Connecticut, 186
suicide, 106

T
Tangipahoa Parish, 183
Tehachapi, California, 148
Thornhill, Ontario, Canada, 177
Toledo, Ohio, 36
Toronto, Ontario, Canada, 61
Tower of London, the, 9
tunnel of light, 163
tunnels between buildings, 33

U
University of Texas, 123

W
White House, the, 9
Wilder, Kentucky, 135
Will Rogers State Park, 194
witch lady, the, 186
Witch of Endor, 81
Wrangell, Alaska, 44

About the Author

Jeff Belanger leads a very haunted life. He's been fascinated with the supernatural since age 10, when he investigated his first haunted house during a sleepover. Since then, he's been a writer and journalist for various newspapers and magazines, and in 1999 he launched Ghostvillage.com as a repository for his writings on the subject of the supernatural. The Web site has since grown to become the largest paranormal community on the Web, attracting hundreds of thousands of visitors per year.

Through Belanger's work as a journalist and a writer, he's had the opportunity to speak with hundreds of people from all over the world regarding the profound events that have changed their lives. His objective and open-minded approach to the subject makes the supernatural accessible to a wide audience. Belanger is a regular guest on many regional and national radio programs, lectures regularly across the United States, and has been featured on television programs about the paranormal. He currently haunts Bellingham, Massachusetts, with his wife, Megan.

Other Books by Jeff Belanger

The World's Most Haunted Places: From the Secret Files of Ghostvillage.com

Communicating with the Dead: Reach Beyond the Grave

Encyclopedia of Haunted Places: Ghostly Locales from Around the World

Ghosts of War: Restless Spirits of Soldiers, Spies, and Saboteurs

The Nightmare Encyclopedia: Your Darkest Dreams Interpreted

12-74